Ancient Links & Future Trails

Egyptian CHARIOT papyrus - Q5 Leap Masterpiece

Remote Viewing: Ancient Links & Future Trails...

The following Remote Viewing treasure hunt includes gems along the way that explain and bring into better focus, precognitive linked Remote View sensing of the Inter-Stellar Trail, designed by God and revealed by this 5th D mapping system. A phenomenon I am calling time vision or simply, timelight. Evolving into SpaceTimeLight (Better dealt with in 'Star Script' www.nuts4mars.com). Along with psi-chi used to paint each Remote View, the viewer feels a certain sense of empathy, as well as precognition, used to guide the focus and tune into the most significant descriptions. In order to draw our attention and impulses to the most necessary in terms of humanity's survival, here on Earth. Perhaps, elsewhere/when is inclusive of other interstellar realms. Here is the Star Trail as mapped and revealed by Remote Viewers, to link to Remote Viewers in our time.

CURRENT UPDATE: August 17, 2009
Re: reading where the Russian disappeared ship was, I said near the top North East of Africa, around the corner from Spain, when I was taking a moment to bother to look at all, for it. They 'found' it within hours of my typing that in. It was South of Spain, off the West coast of Africa, off of Cape Verde.
-For all I know there is some place on the map near Port Said that was a dot to where they were. Who knows, it was not something I was following, I did a stab at it to give them words to look for. Dots they might find useful. I was not drawing an actual 3D map. They insist this has to be 3D. It isn't, it's not even 4D. It's 5D and has a Hypershift. Look at a basic beginner math Necker cube. It shifts from front to back instantaneously. That's a mathematical visual fact.

IN HYPERLAND, Left and Right directions can be reversed. As well as Up being Down. Mostly the codes and emote forms in the psychic paints are read as Descriptives, a lot like the Determinatives of the ancient Egyptian hieroglyphs. The Quantum 5th D often displays this shift! Not always, since the 5th includes the 4th. But laying the trained paints flat and reading them as if the directions revolve 360 degrees, corrects this inherently shifting compass. (note - the understanding and application of Q5 Leap evolved as the Star Trail was worked ceaselessly and developed. Just ignore any errors worked in here, there is just no time as I work the time tunnel during war, to fix it all.)
Do you need to see a Necker cube? Check out Star Script by 1st 5th. I was admitted to the University of Alberta during the days when discovery and progress and research and exploration were all the rage. Or, hey look it up in Dr. Rudolph v.b. Rucker's fine wee classic among the hyperspace set, it's in the Universities' bookstores. It is called (and he has several on the subject) 'Geometry, Relativity and the 4th Dimension' with a full

complete description of the Necker cube and how it relates to inter-dimensionality. Sometimes the front is the front, since the 5th D is inclusive, and descriptive. Audio *and* visual. Sometimes it hyper shifts to the reverse. That is in built. Inherent is a good term for it. Comes with the kit. That's why hyper shift is the base of Teleportation. To put it accurately, the mars race I did was instantaneous or close to, the painting area of the leap to the surface did NOT take 4 minutes to unfold, to paint. It was the entire painting took under 4 minutes and it included far more than just the surface race area and chute etc. it is an instantaneously achieved Hypershift. Near to it, likely one of those neat approaching things like in calculus, a mathematician could work it out for you right down to the details. Already done, for sure. Likely in several different ways. These are Quantum days, not Einstein. They need to catch up or get out of the way. As I say to the other Stargate Viewer working this, Bleep, if they can't do a simple Necker cube they're not even up to high school modern! 9 year olds can do standard Necker cubes. So examining why I thought they had the ship up over Port Said, that's North of the Nile, the Nile was the green for centuries over there, a green river delta, so green and north was south and not the east side, it was the west side. The Port being for ship I guess, that it was due to come to port. They found it in time context or it was anchored and already in a state of like in port. Docked and known. Perhaps. It's about it. And not around the corner, it was straight down, it was a cube shift. Maybe it would help you if I call it a cube shift not the compass rose we were doing romantic hyper shift exploration, revelling in the discovery. These anal retentive don't do anything but linear. Curved, but still linear. They don't do the Hypershift. They are trying to read it flat but only including time, not light. They're not up to speed, as the saying goes. This one goes faster than light speed. Read about the Phoenix Lander Race to Mars using psi versus the Nasa machinery, to see the current confirmation. It's in 'Remote Viewing: Knights of Mars'. It bends light along with time, it is an instantaneous (close to, as in approaching, like they use in calculus) More in 'Imaged 012'. And, get a mathematician and have the *Givens* the 5th parameters. Not the 4th and their rampant misinformation. The ancient Egyptians used addition not multiplication, to arrive at their needs when they were needing a multiplication answer. Read 'Serpent in the Sky' by John Anthony West, for the details. The 5th does that too. It takes individual elements and adds them, you look at them as separate pieces, added like 'dots' together, to make a complete 'visual' or pictograph. It's different way of looking at things, conceptually. So, you can do both, they did more than one interpretation style or level if you like, when reading their 'language' it was visual and audio and …other dimensional capable. Hence the Chariot and its great wealth of holistic connections. A flat hologram. Basically. Now, that is not that hard to understand in todays modern world. If they still can't get it, you need to have them out of there and get in fresh mind unfettered by religious and political override. Some have trouble accepting the 5th. It is like when the Catholic Church locked up Galileo as a Heretic for saying the Earth revolved around the Sun! and they didn't take it back until my own lifetime. They announced that after careful study they had determined it did indeed. No one finds that enlightening guys....it's a standard put down slam to that kind of dino blockage NASA is currently attempting. I say either tune in or go far, far away....

By the sometimes typical reverse order manner, of an extemporaneous nature, I was playing with the developing system many years before this unfolding RV, and in the old work, obscure as it is, as totally visual as it is, (see 'Imaged 0 12') that is where I started to know or sense as it were, the manner of using this system. I recognized it as I found it here, in the papyrus, the 'Chariot' View Theme. And it works, pretty much the same. I think I may of course, not being perfect, missed some, but for the most part, it is a means to find the further extended multi-dimensional platform of coding in the RV Views. We still have to interpret them correctly. Reading these is almost an art form in itself, perhaps why the ancient Egyptians had the words for to hear, to see, to read, to give, in terms of their time tense.

Paintings done by psi directed chi energy enhanced quantum wave packet representations. In other words, creative art paintings, done with an extra psi sense directing them in a highly disciplined chi energy focus. It is fast and comprehensive, complex and capable of great precision. Not meant to replace God; it is not perfect. The process results in fascinating Pre-Cog Remote Views that link to other View Themes and other Viewers. During this present time and in ancient times as well…

'ddt' what he gives (present); 'rdit.n' what he gave (past); 'rdity.f' one who may/will give (future); *one who may/will hear, one who may/will see; they had one for 'read' Remote Views sometimes come out all mix and match, bits and pieces combining, superimposing, to present a coded message. Stories to unravel in their own good time. Like articles in a container jumbled together, and then reassembled. Offering only glimpses of their original design or intent. With moments and overall View Themes of exquisite precision.

 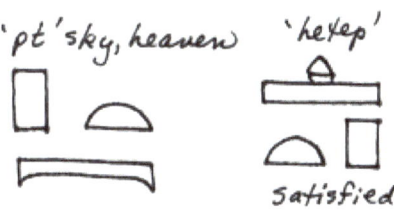

'Sky; heaven' Remote View, 2001; Egyptian hieroglyph 'he tep, peace, satisfaction.

    There is another one, using the determinative for sky, only with a star hanging down under it. Must be the Aussies, in the coalition forces, Down Under. They have a thing called a walk about, I think it is. The walker theme, for army, maybe, and luke sky walker for the air force. Part of this conflict, as a determinative marker. It could be Dingo Star, aka Info. A Dingo is an Australian wild dog.

    Egyptian hieroglyphs for sky, or heaven. Read left to right, phonetically sounds like 'pet'. In ancient Egypt people went to the priests of Anubis for a glance into the future. Maybe it surfaced today because that is a future time jumper team. Like a successful termination of the great evil one, Usama bin Laden.

Older plane tail match to ancient Egyptian hieroglyph RV theme

    When you're reading the hieroglyphs, the scholarly interpreters don't seem to have found vowels, so they just add the sound of 'e', not a hard e. It is like in 'pet' in-between all the letters you sound out. May help explain why my older map of Iraq, and Baghdad uses 'e's instead of the 'I's that they use in place names now on maps, or in the media, anyway. In ancient Egyptian belief, a sparrow, or similar bird, is a noisy, agitated, destructive creature that reproduces endlessly. Found at the end of words belonging to the category of what is bad, small, weak and it is called the bird of evil.

    These next two ancient Egyptian hieroglyphic works both of which exhibit straightforward characteristics of Remote View Themes linking to this Time Context. As discovered, explored and deciphered, using skill and persistence. The one below is a carving from a Temple in Abydos, Egypt, by ancient Egyptians.

1. (Abydos) Ancient Egyptian hieroglyphic carving; certain Remote Viewing Mastership.

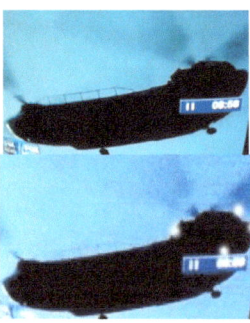

Remote View visual links between the Abydos carving and the present conflicts' helicopter air ships: 2008 Black Hawk U.S. military helicopter; Afghanistan, Apache Gun Ship; Chinook helicopter Afghanistan 2008. A few RV theme components, in dots.
The (left) helicopter tail angles in dots, are reversed in the Abydos carving's angles.

'Kingdom of the Crystal Skull' starring Harrison Ford, RV crossing time leap lines, with an old plane style a possible match to the tail, if the curve is reversed 180 degrees, as per RV Compass Rose effect; RV mix & match precision visual components; tank RV; (end) View of elongated skull from movie

2. Ancient Egyptian 'Chariot' Papyrus Remote View Theme

3. Chariot papyrus, mathematically precise description of the *tangent point*, as pertaining to the hyper-shift involved in the Remote Viewing process. Starting at the hand, and running a line to the lower orb, forming a tangent, it co-aligns nicely with the arrow as it is placed in the bow. Here describing the dynamics of aim and direction.

The ancient Egyptians' depth of understanding of the process of Pre-Cog Remote Viewing was extraordinary. Perhaps it was the clarity of a less cluttered time. Especially this particular ancient Egyptian Pre-Cog View Theme. A precision masterpiece, in terms of Remote Viewing, and a match to present day military craft.

The conflicts in the ancient land of Mesopotamia for the main security and survival concerns during these times. Naturally these are also then, the concerns of the Pre-Cog artistry. With psi directing the connections, resulting in these matching visuals. The ancient tablet describing military craft from *now*.

Clearly the ancient Egyptians were accomplished with the visual Pre-Cog method of recording psi leaps according to quantum principles, today commonly known as Pre-Cog Remote Views. Following View Themes presented by the creative talent linked to such qualitative works as 'Minority Report' starring Tom Cruise, focusing on Pre-Cog, and 'the 5th Element' with Bruce Willis, revealing the necessity of empathic elements linking to extend beyond. Going beyond the timelight barrier into an inter-dimensional experience of elsewhere/when involving SpaceTimeLight.

I had an amazing surprise, as a functioning Pre-Cog Remote Viewer, doing reconnaissance between 2006 and 2008, Planet Earth and Mars, using psi. I found during my de-coding and empathic linking, two ancient previous recordings done by Masters of Remote Viewing. Two visuals, one a story on a papyrus and the other a carved tablet, both written by ancient Egyptian Viewers and revealing specifically. Linking specifically to our current times. What I call the 'Time Context' of a View Theme (the tale that decodes). Each individual view contains accurately recorded precision markers.

Patterns become discernable, with a sense of overall tension or cohesion, to form rare delightful glimpses linked to a time else when as well as current. A crystal ball delicacy of tuned Oracle windows. Glimpses from the world of the Cheshire cat. Achingly reflective of teleportation, time travel, and interstellar adventures. Remote Views opening a trail along a quantum edge, the 5th D. Ultra sensational, absorbing, piercing the timelight barrier. Views contain future content, like the previews of upcoming features, at the beginning of a dvd. The trailers. maybe that's what they did in the pyramids, hung out and Viewed. They might have been tuning into select stars. I would not rule it out, from having personally experienced this. Makes sense. To connect to stars. And then to the life forms surrounding them. Most likely the significance of the triangle, implicit in my use of three similar spheres, and three for planet 3, that's us, and the ship is the solar energy source, the sun, in that regards. Descriptive. Like the use of the Determinative, by Egyptologists.

Using the concept of triangulation, as a part of following star trails. You don't go to the planet, you tune into solar systems. A lot of star systems are binary, with elliptical interwoven orbits. Stars dance around each other. It is necessary to have a View ability to facilitate the compass rose effect. It's early, I explained it later I think. And the strange but ever fascinating effect of having the very structure of our language on Earth, encompassing Time Vision. The ancient roots of the languages not just Egyptian hieroglyphs but also traces in very early Elamite, Celtic, Easter Island (Rongo Rongo), and the Indus Valley, to name a few. I have explored some connections that apply directly in this **distinctly View 5th in-between manner** further along. Like the rest of this, the meanings and messages, decoding as they go along, unfolding their cryptic little jewels. Like finding stars in Deepside. And from the stars, the planet oases surrounding them.

   The two Egyptian pieces I have been following while operating as an Oracle, are extremely phenomenological in nature. For the through the X-Streme Stargate door Views', fleeting glimpses of elsewhere/when, call it Time Vision if you like.

   Only, not so fleeting. Decoding the treasure-map Views' markers, I have found it links exquisitely by 5th-D leaps, through included time tunnel decoding instructions as to going into hyper-shift Remote View leaps. With chances of this being probably to hopefully certainly, interstellar in design. And perhaps even more astonishing, linking between our Time
Context and the ancient Remote Viewers ' own. Trust me, they had more than one Viewer.

Enlarged snip from Chariot papyrus; descriptive of superluminal motion, in dots

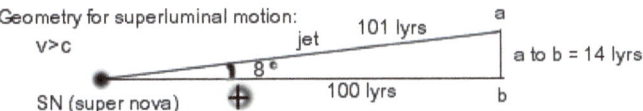

at ⊕ source seems to have moved from b to a (d=14 lys) in only 1 year

implies transverse speed of 14 c (c= speed of light)

v= 2c/sin 8°=2c/.1391731 =2(3x10to8thm/s)/.1391731 =4.311x10to9th)m/s

Example of superluminal geometry. As for the 4 dots on the orb (above), it would visually describe rotation, wouldn't you think? And if you look at the diagram above, the a to b is moving, it is a part of a rotating circular line, an orbit, not a linear anything, really.

Describing an optical illusion called superluminal motion where light is faster than c; given that this is in an ancient Egyptian hieroglyphic visual (hence using *determinatives*) of a Remote View, this would be *descriptive* of the actual process. Timelight is indeed faster than 'c' over normal distance range, in our normal dimensional limits. However beyond the barrier this is obviously no longer true as a realistic block. Quantum doesn't behave in a strictly linear manner. My evidence is plenty, my proof is astounding.

Ancient Egyptian hieroglyphs are a natural for passing along visual and multi-layered meanings. They use a system designed to be read by not only looking at the language as it is written, but also containing within it, a way to raise up to another level. Like a computer program that provides links to other levels. These are enabled here, by following along a trail of masterful and well defined connections. Once you know how to get these points marked and then connected accurately. Upon reviewing the reset links another layer of imagery and meaning becomes apparent. This is a visual language complete with Remote Viewing being taken into account. Viewing was not seen as some strange, bizarre and frightening boogey man apparition. Rather, it was included with deliberation and dedication, as the ancient renderings were carved out. It appears ancient Egyptian hieroglyphs were meant not only as a visual language but also as a *Vision* language.

According to the tale in the ancient Egyptian papyrus I call the 'Chariot', they had trouble with the ancient roots of the Muslim men's Terrorist Cult, too. Perhaps not so much carrying over into our times, as having been re-invented.
Shooting out with such definite and certain aim towards another star system. And they waved back! given the following account where it explains who these ancient pieces of Time Vision, these are likely concerned with describing quantum phenomena. A wave singularity, like Or, hand signal within range indicators, or signal range, and the D, for inter- dimensional. You can see the hand's tip, at the left dipping into the next body. Visually submerged or immersed within or under, another layer. Likely signifying another dimension given this ability deals with hyper-shift and it's multidimensionality quality.

In this current Time Context piece, note the dark semi-to-circular Mickey Mouse's ear tip, on the 2nd finger of the waving-hand. From back when, if you remember the old standard Mickey Mouse waved his hand like that. The Saudis. They are determining now, what is allowed within their code of behaviour range. If they had not just said they wanted Mickey Mouse killed because he was one of Satan's Soldiers. Look at the fringe people. Alongside in this view range. They're **up** to *something*, I tell you. It was on the 'Jurassic Park ' movie series by Michael Crichton, 'Lost World' poster. Something. Look at the bottom it says, *Something*.

 Chariot papyrus RV theme (snip enlarged from 'Chariot'); two hands determining range, defining distance and the rather hand-waving-like structure in between them.

 A glimpse beyond the Veil, as and when provided by a fond Lord, clearly as a guiding light on our path. In fact you can find rather frequent reference to prophecy in the Holy Bible. Especially in regards to a passage which actually once revealed, lifts quite a bit of the Veil in regards to the Open Stargate.

 A symbolically important military hand over in Iraq took place in this related Time Context. The hand on the left, that submerges, also means within. The speaker's hand went inside the top covering of the cabinet set up to hold notes on the podium, and was covered from the audience's sight. Showing it has meaning within our regular 4th D too. You can see that as an inverted white flag shape, triangular on top at the side of a pole. Perhaps given the Context, it would indicate the surrender of the enemy, their loss in Iraq facilitating the removal of additional troops from over there, and the changing of the top commanders involved.

 Nowadays, in terms of this Open Stargate, you could perhaps consider it a combination of the Tom Cruise movie 'Minority Report' water immersed Pre-Cog blended together with a movie, 'Jumper' (older) and Google visuals, for precise co-ordinate experience only in terms of Hypershift and the 5th. Using Inter-Galactic Psi!

 A View from within the **TT** or Time Tunnel often involves looking from above and descending down through layers of visual and empathic impressions forming the View.

 The ancient Egyptians had a deity called **Anubis**. He was the **god of the night and of those who would see into the future**. Another title for Anubis, this god who could see into the future, was 'the one who is upon his mountain'. A visual perspective from above, looking down. Their language being intertwined with Remote Viewing visuals.

 Egyptian hieroglyphs for intuition, moon; visually, like the diagram for v>c optical illusion in 'Dancing Wu Li Masters' by Gary Zukav go to page 142 for it. Usually that would be random and insignificant, but the subject matter this has revealed as it was deciphered with Remote View links, makes it a possible for a visual description, a likely RV theme. Mysterious as that is.

Including the top left eye, it is 4 eyes and 4 tusks within this RV set, visual 'frame'

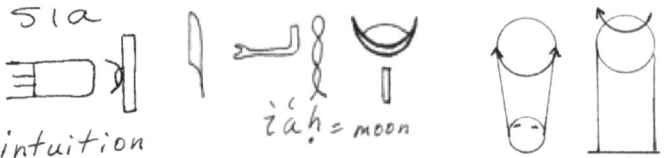

Gist of Visual for v>c optical

    Above, the cross arrangement of 4, presents to me in its time context, the concept that using 4 dots in a cross pattern presents the outline with a small dark spot in between them making a central dot placement position. Good for the sensed tension, or overall dynamics. Where such placement could be initiated as a direct stimulus to place it there such as by intuition. Or, it could be at other times the result of an additional connection point being introduced as you follow along the already pre-determined guidelines (see 'Imaged 012') for sensing, finding and placing points of interest. Done within a time frame of its own essential condition of 'the present'. They can then be seen as dots or line defining form within, or seen as outlines around something, as well as by positive and negative space effects. And, usually can be read or interpreted either as visually precise - thus revealing a complete rendering of an item or form. Or the more often formed snippets of RV scrobbling, lines and spirit, empathic cohesive wave units etc. to be read and understood in a more certainly *descriptive* manner. An RV theme describes a 'to be' and/or a 'was' as well as is, in terms of time tense accompanying any Remote View. Very Shakespeare, and 'The Postman' by David Brin, who also advised NASA on astrophysics, interestingly enough. Funny how remote viewing links to Star Trails.

    Sort of a quantum mass Reality meter for a common experience. In a way you could say it was the ship all of Earth's creatures ride along together in. It is how we perceive and understand Reality. Our individual linking up to the greater 5th Dimension. Otherwise it would all be just one big mish mash, an indecipherable smash of color and sensation. Items and objects, states and events are given names, description and definition. In order for us to be able to link to a common reality, a quantum hold. There would be a universal in the literal meaning, language form enabled by this means.

Descriptive of shared physical parameters and determinatives, such as distance, light and speed. Perhaps to link together others of similar form. It's a thought. It could be the still or freeze frame we all access into. I guess you could call it a mainframe. The holistic nature of the Universe . Ours in these times seems to me, could use an injection of truth about the 5th Dimension glimpsed by Remote Viewers. And no, I am not the First Remote Viewer, only the first to lay claim to being the first to Mars, during any Race to the Planet's surface, and accomplished at a speed greater than c., as well as remarkably enough, through a Leap through elsewhere/when. As evidenced by the earlier painting, the 'Face On Mars'. Quantum psi experience that this is. (see the Phoenix Lander pages in 'Remote Viewing: Knights of Mars'.) Kevin Costner, the hunk of the moment in the foreground. Go Kev! He starred in the movie 'The Postman'. Another creative talent Remote View link. And all on the trail to the stars, once you connect the dots….

Using tension (dynamics) to determine placement; resulting in tip of hand to tip of arrow inter-linear precision alignment. Incredibly enough.
The diagram is a visually descriptive match to view objects in the moon/intuition hieroglyphic arrangement. The explanation he gives concerns a faster than light visual illusion caused by looking down from above, and rotating the ball very fast. Again, hieroglyphs link directly to references which allude to superluminal motion.

   An entirely different matter than a military, or others, use according to their own skill in reading these Views to glean useful information from. They are not trying to leave a legacy of prophecy, linking Remote and Wizard Views together for meaning in Time Context. In a current application, these View paintings basic spy sheets, pretty much. They are highly descriptive and depend on interpretation. Like breaking a code, repeatedly. As for accuracy in outcome from consulting one, you get what you get, no promises. This isn't some guaranteed life mechanism. No Holy Grail for individual immortality. Perhaps, a trail to the immortal stars.

Ancient Chinese brushwork and Oracles, share with the Egyptian hieroglyphs remarkable sense of spirit as well as advanced technique. Vision Language that includes the 5th-D. We get to see and decipher the past and the links to the trail that is the most promising into the future. The stimulated emission mentioned here is the chi energy at the behests of the empathy. Of course, since I am not a laser or a maser. In meditative disciplines, the use of focused energy and concentration to rise into a state of heightened awareness, or super-psi, would be it's equivalent. Actually, some of the ancient meditation symbols were fashioned very much the same as the base I used when developing precognition using intuitive logic. Symbols being ancient archetypes as well as being incorporated into our modern but still human, selves. Brain waves or microwaves, it's all just waves. What they call quantum wave packets, just photo pack reality.

Chariot papyrus Remote View hunt theme; alignment alongside the line and point of the arrow tip; sightline ends at front black hooded image with dotted white eyes

This RV particularly matched to a lady at a pump in Afghanistan. An illusion of snake eyes by dots along a black cloth covering loosely thrown up across her face, Afghanistan, 2008. Visually, it looked the same as the black hood with the two white dots for eyes found at the end of the straight line, computer drawn and precise, lined up alongside the arrow's tip. The hieroglyph of an owl and leg/hoof means 'repeat'.

Specifically, an author wrote a book called 'Futility', about a ship called the Titan that had a slightly shifted but similarly detailed descriptive View Theme, of the very real, and very huge disaster, the sinking of the Titanic.

Titanic photo; Chariot Remote View headpiece visual, match to tips of smokestacks and tops of pillars

This specific View Theme seems to have already played out. It could link descriptively, to another View time. You woudn't want to rule that possibility out, entirely. As a caution. Notice the portholes match, too. There are details online at: http://paranormalinsider.com/2008/04/titanic_disaster_prophesized. Php

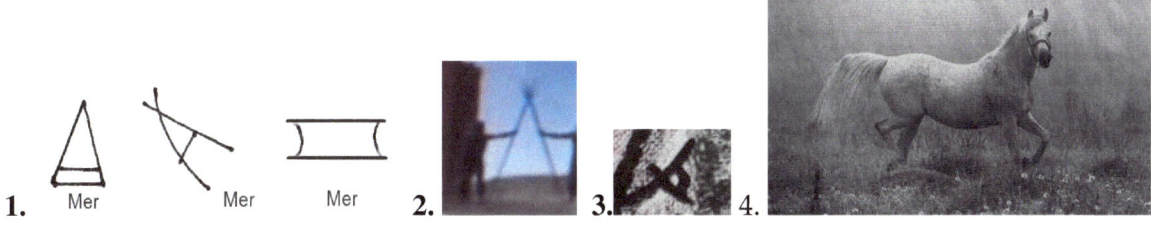

1. ancient Egyptian hieroglyph lines for 'Mer'; match to 2. tall spears 3. RV pattern, of sticks in the bush, building a survival shelter 4. match horse legs/under belly forms

'Mer' Egyptian hieroglyphic patterns; match to the empty spaces formed by horse's legs, and under its belly, between the legs. The Mer lines above, are easy to see in this photo of a horse standing in a field, near Winnipeg, Canada. (photo, *Journal*).

In 'Lord of the Rings' by J.R.R. Tolkien, the author also seems to create with links to certain Remote Views. For example, Aragorn as goes before them with the Flame of the West; he is called foresighted and timely. And a white horse caught my eye, like the one in the movie 'Pathfinders'. The legs forming mer patterns in a similar horse, standing still in a field. In ancient Egyptian hieroglyphs, mer meant to love. Merlin's Wizardry myth is based on love, the 5th element. That unseen mysterious force that is essential to being human and distinguishes us from ghoul creatures.

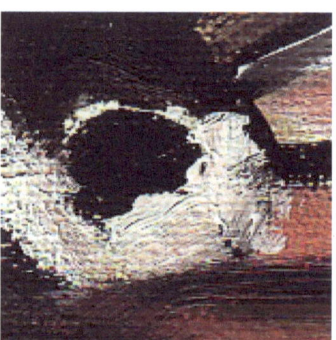

Remote View 2007; artifact bottom right, enlarged; Jesus Ossuary (Israel Antiquities Authority) recently discovered; RV Chariot wheel pattern match, 2006

    Beside the Jesus ossuary is the wheel excerpt from the ancient Egyptian Chariot papyrus. You can clearly see the positioning of the wheel struts or angles, is a match to the first symbol on the Jesus box. Also, as an additional indicator, the wheel has a double outer line, and the symbol on the box is within a circle, and again describes an inner circle to that one. And the double parallel lines, in the center of the box, are marked on the wheel by corresponding parallel lines formed on the top right, inner wheel-described within the first 45 degrees from the horizontal. With a row of dots running along within these parallel lines. A match to the markers of the dots running along on the Jesus box, only they are running along the outside of the parallel lines there, and within the parallel lines on the wheel. (The initial page in my poetry book 'Myst' has the same dot formations, inside the center circles of the wheel. Formed by following the system imaged and explored visually, in 'Imaged 012' included on CD).

    At the base of the Jesus box is a little like a foot, or rest, that you can make out a front part showing. A small rectangle at each end. Bottom right hand side of the wheel, is a similar empty space describing the same small rectangular shape. Perhaps the damage in the lower left, to the form by the flowers in the wheel.

    If not probable at least possible, with the establishment of water on Mars, that the speculation could turn to the four circular orbs (removed) in the original Christian Cross form, was meant to indicate (or, by virtue of Remote Viewing, sense), a fourth planet out from the sun, Mars.

You can clearly see the round depressions along the top of the figure, indicating there were once four circles. And if you look closely you can see perhaps, a slight indication that the inner form may have been also surrounded with repeat patterning, (the base for the prevailing method of artistic creation by means of a heavy reliance on sheer repetition, of the region's culture, to come? They might have been trying to replicate the Love energy that came with Christ. Don't forget, the term for praise is also the symbol the ancient Egyptians used for the beneficial energy, that they used a repeat form visual hieroglyph for.

It looks like the outer extended repeat pattern shapes were maybe the hexagon shaped forms, made by placing lines along the inner triangles, you know, like on the Jesus Box. The same treatment of the wheel. And you get the shape of the Hypersquare, its outline. And yes, sure enough, if you look closely inside the center star form in its circle, at the top, along the intersection points of the triangle and the circle, you can indeed make out the straight lines forming these outer hyper square edges. It is there. I am not 'hallucinating' on beans. Planet Earth always is fascinating. The cross in the circle describes an intersection, or point at the center of a circle.

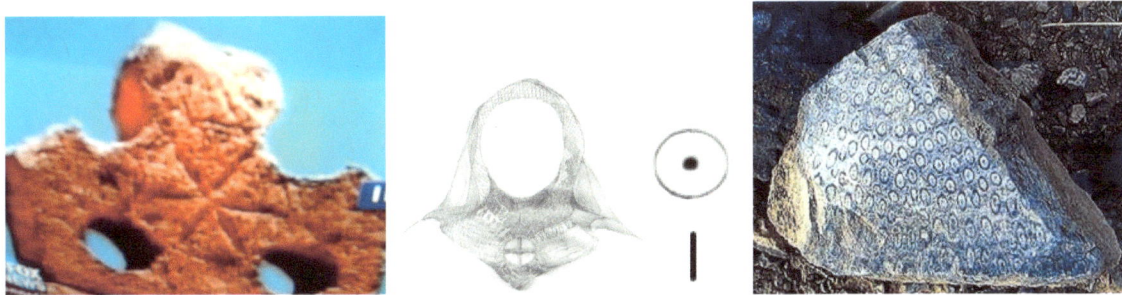

Christian carved cross; head covering RV; hieroglyph Ra-Sun; Sun symbol rock

Earliest Christian church Jordan, note the round outer circle around the crossed lines, with complete triangles rendered within. Harness mounts found in Southern England, 200 AD show similar markings. Pencil work, foretelling RV and X-Streme Stargate, to me. (online) rock covered in sun circles. Counting days; orbits, of the sun and the moon. Orbits are clearly a view from above, or **Earthside** knowledge. Not just earthbound views of a sun. That they were describing **Earthside** Viewing is a remarkable but tangible conclusion. Visually, it could be descriptive RV of a modern day CD/DVD.

'Hunt' '94; Shuttle; Gomez's Hamburger Nebula, match to RV 'Hunt' inside ship; 'ned' an unknown Egyptian hieroglyph

 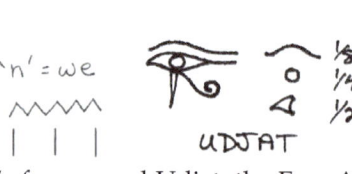 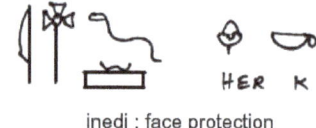

'End Time Angel' 1997; hieroglyph's for we and Udjat, the Eye; As fractions, the vertical line is 1/64th and the curved bottom line with the curled end, is 1/32nd

The ancient RV visual hieroglyph for the word, 'ned', as an unknown. Could be a clean energy wind tower. Mysterious as most RV is, the word 'ned' was in the also very strange movie '23' starring Jim Carrey. He also did the 'Truman Show'. Capturing life in this isolated timetravel capsule, (I just need to put a sign on my door…) watching the rest of the world in my laptop under their (and they think *I'm* weird) continuous monitoring system. See what other little goodies they may have picked up on and pointed to. That is supposed to be a feather, but you know it could be a knife too. The cutting edge often revealed by the truth. Whew, turns out it was linked to a dove's breast, too.

    The following is a Remote Viewer reading, using my super tuned senses of course, of this hieroglyphic arrangement on protection. Given the preceding explanations relating to the modern links to the ancient Pre-Cog Remote Views, the message being rather explicit. With an open mind, the imagery connects to modern patterns recognized by our senses. Sight *and* sound. And a currently unidentified hieroglyph, in the term for protectors. Protectors or punishers?

    I have laid out here how specific ancient hieroglyphs contain message content that links by means of precognition to our modern times. And, also, how to follow along using a system of decoding. A fascinating trail in itself. My super sleuthing turning up little gems of treasure along the star trail. Some good, some not so good, nonetheless necessary as warnings, so the good will prevail.

    Could be the aiming of the arrow in the Chariot into the corner, near the Golden Orb, as a sun form, a precise visual. The sun does indeed look like a golden orb. Combined with the way the diagram matches it, for the superluminal graphic. Appearing described as a 'back at you' process. So, from the sun, reformulated, back into the sun, as sunform. Natural sun energy or nuclear, energy wasteland. Just be careful, the WormWood warning has already played through. Since Wormwood was the literal translation of the word Chernobyl, and they already had their nuclear incident. And caused a radioactive wasteland as a result.

A reversed from right top to lower left, X, Y, Z…the Y and Z outlining the ground and air of the pyramid shape, and the X marking a spot in the sky, the inner chambers of the pyramid of Giza, the alignment to the stars probably signified here in this visual. Their star points. Like in the 'the Last Crusade', 'X' again marks the spot. As well as linking to the roots of our own modern alphabet, the Chariot visuals also show striking connections to the ancient Elamite, Middle Eastern script. Like the snippet included here.

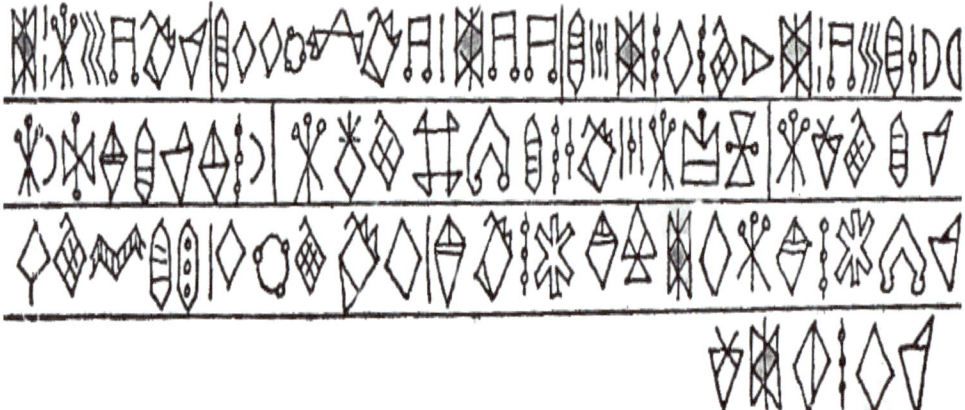 Elamite script

Remote View 2006; view looking down from above on one of the world's oldest ships, desert March 2006 (online); Elamite (SW Iran) ancient script ship shape; match to this letter reversed in the 'Book of Kells', (page 55); Easter Island *Rongo Rongo* script triangular ship with a top mast; top right corner or Elamite script above, the visual for an in-between Wormhole, denoting Range, match to Egyptian term for range, albeit they use them at their horizontal not vertical.

₁ ₂ ₁ ₂ ₂ ₃

Voynich (left, 1), match to Elamite (Iran, right, 2); 3 Egyptian 'range'

'Book of Kells' excerpt; 3 markers; Voynich center /ship image; linear, 2D plane

('Book of Kells' page 55) top right enlarged, visual match to Elamite script boat letter; (page 18) ships/orbs; descriptive meaning 'water globe/world'; Earth from space, note curved dark shadow region (between dots) like the orbs on the circumference of the ships circle from the page next to it.

 Visual markers are highly symbolic, and can be interpreted on multi-visual levels. Literally as well, since the ('Book of Kells' page 18)orbs arranged along the outer edge of the ship-circle-form or 'water globe/world' show sunlight moving over the Earth as it revolves, as seen from a space view looking towards Earth.

 There are clear links between the 'Book of Kells' and the ancient visual languages, both Elamite and Egyptian. And linking thus via the small boat, and the RV certainty of the cover selection, to the odd Voynich manuscript.

 Ships and planet Earth from an Earthside perspective, looking down from inter-planetary Space towards the Earth, and watching the sun play out over it as it revolves. I saw that at the start of a movie the other day. I forget what it was. water world maybe. I still think it is unfolding as a warning. We need to develop those hyper shift and teleport friendly star trails. If the polar caps melt, this planet is water world, you would want to prepare. The View Theme of the Oops! This Planet Floods. And it isn't just in Hollywood. There are also Comets. One might have taken out Planet X…where all the asteroids float around instead….and it is littered all over Mars. We have no idea what was or could be or is, out there…star trek set about the right attitude, actually. Exploration, development, embracing the marvellously new.

'Book of Kells' page 41, enlarged match to ancient script
http://nabataea.net/writingch.html ; Egyptian hieroglyphic for 'T' is a Rectangle shape

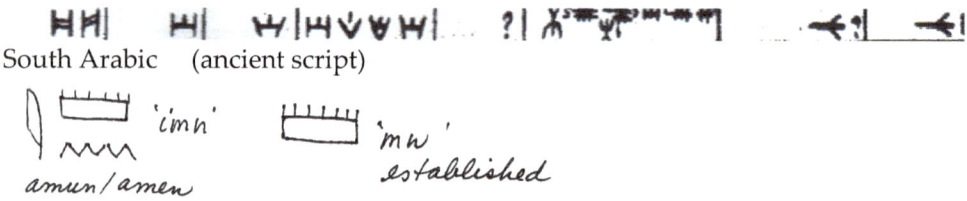
South Arabic (ancient script)

'imn' amun/amen
'mn' established

Amen, a customary prayer ending; visual implies distance, near to far away

'Book of Kells' page 41; Iraqis Military success June 30/09 key presentation match to the symbol below, the Egyptian 'tie'; same symbol showing in Medieval engravings Castle lore (end plate)

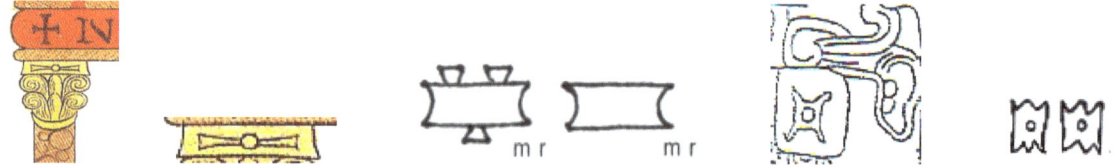

Post tops, match to Egyptian hieroglyph for 'tie' inside 'mer', above 'moon'; Egyptian hieroglyph for 'mer' here, can mean canal, visual link to laptop latches, 2 back, 1 front & the latch on the end of the ancient S. Arabic script line; with the 3 markers, road or Way; Mayan symbol; Easter Island *Rongo Rongo* script with a similar form (above, at far right end)

ancient script, S. Arabic, left

   See the colour picture plates in 'Mayan Prophecies' by Maurice Cotterell, specifically the Mayan Lid of Palenque with the matching curls of flow like Kells ('Book of Kells' page 41) illumination visuals pillar-tops to an old script letter; similar Easter Island's Rongo Rongo script letter.

   So, what does all this interconnectedness relate to in terms of a message. Vision Language is first and foremost a communication devise. Flight, seems to be the order of the day. Travel, roadways, encompassing multi-dimensional as well as linear methods.

   A lot of RV is concerned with empathically linking words, recognizing patterns, colors, places, hints, clues, portents, snippets. All done as quantum snooping. My discovery being the connection of the ancient Vision Language, as determined by the modern Pre-Cog Views. It seems that predominantly, the Views link to this specific Time Context because of the intense nature of the conflict our civilization is concerned with. Our current hunt for the terrorists linking to the ancients' hunts as well, via the View component within senses.

  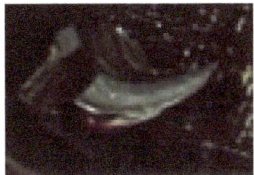

Chariot View, sea diver articles; submarine, 2008 An enlarged snip, of a sharp tooth, (bottom right, reversed image); similar tooth under the bottom of the gold orb in the top left of this snippet enlarged from the Chariot papyrus

Israelis F-16I superimposed images; wheel snip- center, 4 stems

Still photo of reactor falling; RV pre-event; Chariot View snip; cooling towers, cracks

As you can clearly observe, this is an ancient Egyptian Pre-Cog View Theme visual match to the destruction of the nuclear reactor towers in Pyong Yang as a direct result of the intervention of the World community and their desire to stop nuclear weapons programs. A strongly positive sign on the road to global conditions of peace for all of us, together. Placed in their View Theme to mark the occasion as significant.

Things jump around in the time lane, elsewhere/when comes into play. That's why I like to call it time traveling, since the Pre-Cog does views of either the past or the present or the future, or some that have connections to describe a condition relevant to all/or others, too. I think he is tuning on the outside, rather than on the inside. Maybe like the difference between plugging something in for electricity/energy compared to using wireless. One is outside and one is inside, descriptively. The instances of not happening, may just be the cat box opened somewhere else. A teleport effect involved.

First line goes from the final outcome position, lower right corner, 1. Eye to 2. Hand Representing eye hand coordination, line of sight, using extended parallels/diagonals; or as symbolized by the 'X' and the '\ \' in their hieroglyphics, read in terms of RV.

    These are pointers, cosmic indicators if you care to tune in. Taken a lot for granted nowadays, to lots of people, to be able to do things, sensitively. That's how this works like being able to recognize a color on sight. But not fine tuning sound or sight, in his case maybe fine tuning some pre-existing psi-energy wave muscle. Unlike the meditators or psychics approach, coming from within, maybe this is more using the outside constructs to achieve a tuning. Psi-chi, as quantum possible.

    I have some training in logic and abstraction through philosophy. This process consists of intuitive-logic combined with natural empathy and psi talent. Seeking solutions and the lights along our star trail. Earth's future as foreordained. Like I said, this is the crossroads, and you need to start helping them to find a solution. It is a time of great need, great division. Organized, and like a bad spell, potent within their duration.

    Usually, the moon gets pegged as cool for the psychic emoting. Emotions and ulterior motives and agendas will cloud and muck up the picture with guided emotion. Linking intersection points and overlap, following his own lines, it looks like Da Vinci was Remote Viewing the pyramid structure they built in front of the Louvre Check out this visual of it at the Louvre's website.

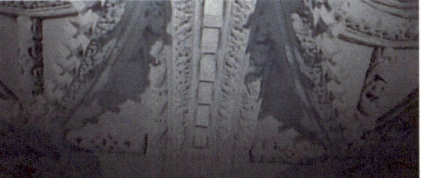 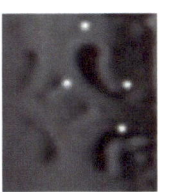 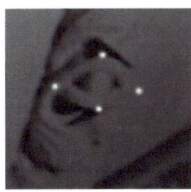

Ceiling, Rosslyn Chapel; ear (ceiling left) and eye (right), photo: Jonathan Greet(www.dumdum.co.uk) http://www.panoramas.dk/da-vinci-code/rosslyn-chapel.html

 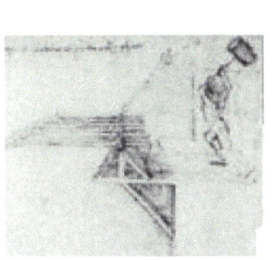 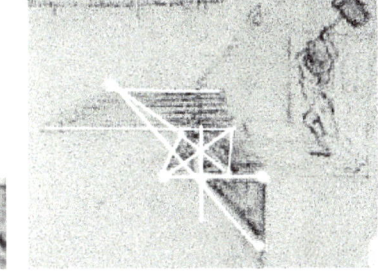

Drawings by Leonardo Da Vinci; using same system of forming links as other ancient Remote Viewing links (see ebook 'Imaged 012' for additional explanation on the system); Da Vinci Tarot, psi selected Da Vinci drawings; RV system of applying white dots/lines; Note, again, the parallels and the diagonal providing a visual link or connecting bridge between levels.

Pencil 1983, my RV; Da Vinci, don't look at me for strange check out how he was *fading in and out*

 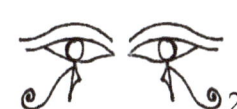 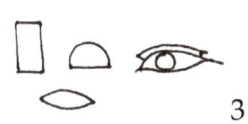 

1. The eye, Udjat, with defined areas of measure; 2. The Falcon Eyes marking for View; 3. 'ptr', to observe (the single eye determinative at the end, 'ir') 4. Remote View pen/ink

You can see the striations of the visual and a fairly decent descriptive match overall. And netted into the structure of the remote view connecting overlaps, tangents and planes. Using additional measures and means, such as gaps, extensions, layering, superimposing, etc. there are several things in the connect-all-kit to reading these things. The leap of faith is required, not optional.
http://www.louvre.fr/llv/pratique/alaune.jsp?bmLocale=en and the Da Vinci drawings are from a Tarot deck, http://www.aeclectic.net/tarot/ www.aeclectic.net/tarot/ebooks/
Unlike the clarity of RV and other vision means, the psychic clairvoyant. Hence the term crystal ball for accuracy of Vision. You want a nice clean crystal for Reading. Nowadays, with our profusion and overwhelming population complexity, it is easier to Remote View on other planets and use the ancient papyrus and other tantalizing windows the former Remote Viewer's left behind. This volume here, is likely for the future Viewers. I am most aware of this.

Faithfully tapping into the 5th D and otherness of things, and the time frame of 'now' are likely becoming more and more consciously aware of the threads that are showing. With the connections becoming more obvious.

For the 'Da Vinci' set following along after Dan Brown's inspiration, here is from the very ceiling of the Rosslyn Chapel (The Compass/Blue Rose and Time Vision Timeline? Likely. Knowing what I do, make that probably.

'Confucius says about this line: The hawk is the object of the hunt; bow and arrow are the tools and means. The marksman is man (who must make proper use of the means to his end0. The superior man contains the means in his own person. He bides his time and then acts. Why then should not everything go well? He acts and is free. Therefore all he has to do is to go forth and he takes his quarry. This is how a man fares who acts after he has made ready the means.' I Ching oracle, An Oracle is a gift designed to help with the keeping of life. Pre-Cog is meant to be freely exchanged between oracles.

Most, if not all, of my former creative oil paintings were actually Remote Views. That includes the dimension of Time, ahead of time. The paintings from then, match up with current events. Often either space or military events. This is after all, the Time Context of Now. And those are the most crucial areas in terms of our survival. Mostly what Remote Viewing ability is for.

Stargate Remote View, movie '10,000 B.C.' Steven Strait, Cliff Curtis; 'bow' in dots

Long-Bow View, outlined by (randomly placed visual aids only) dots, 2008

There is no evil eye with this painting. The eye was with the tree, with the cables connection. Signals for communication. And as for the super twist being found adapted from ancient Egypt to the Catholic church, gee, go figure. Since Constantine of Rome, was the inventor of what to keep and what to discard when they made the manmade form of what they pass off on us as their version of Christianity. And the reason for the meeting to finalize the form of Christian worship, was because they had too many gods and goddess going way back. So, they retained some of the heathen or original celebrations and considerations. That symbol represents the worship of the sun as the creator symbol.

They also kept Christmas, etc. and all Christian church prayer ends with the words Amen. Amen -Ra (Ra being the Sun) was from Ancient Egypt, too. It was Akhen-Aten who tried to get them to do away with the multitude of gods and goddesses and worship one God only. The same structure underlying Christianity was even earlier initiated from within ancient Egypt. A pre- Constantine reformation of the main priority of a religious matter of faith. Constantine was the back when Ruler responsible for combining the pagans with their belief in multi-deities, with the Church; ultimately bringing religious beliefs under one umbrella of practice, Christianity, with one God. Unlike the Egyptian attempt to switch to monotheism, this one succeeded. Along with the certain inclusion of some of the original humankind ancient tales and traditions. An example of the ability of legends staying afloat, carried along by the will of the people. It was not the first time Earth's people superseded one God over the concept of the many. You can't pretend they are only concerned with evil and the Devil when they are also the origin of the concept of the worship of God.

Lower right corner of Chariot papyrus, shape/time link to patch and hair (der Herr), movie 'Valkyrie', starring Tom Cruise, Remote View Ace, for View Lord ('Egyptian Art' hieroglyphic)

Just like time is now understood to be part of our experience of space. Hence we now know space/time as a base condition for our experiencing reality. In all sentient forms life requires both physical and spiritual connections. Otherwise, we would be no better than emotionless soul-less robots or rocks. The inclusion of the fifth as a significant dimension, is necessary in order for us to realize the preciousness of Life itself. Within this reality. The ability to dynamically involve the 5th Dimension distinguishes us from a robot that succeeds in space/time, requiring 4 dimensions, but fails in Life, requiring 5 dimensions. This wondrous 5th of course defining all living creatures, not merely humans. Now, must mean we get to go interstellar and not stuck in Marxville. Not fashionable, like hair blobs? Could be. No, really. Herr meaning Master, a gentleman, herrlich- glorious, beautiful. Haar is hair.

So, the visual matches his hair blob. The way things work? And he did get the Mars thing however that worked. And he is bang on for this ss for RV theme. And I thought he was out to lunch on it when he started it, but nope, bang on. He must work hard. Very hard. So, yeah, probably an RV marker. And the book getting some notice, so, it is out front …oh I think it is more, it has a dark line attached to it, that runs along the dogs snout, I don't know what it is. There is a row of dots, like the comets, so maybe as a marker meaning interplanetary, or earthside space, like...outer space. Call it. And 'alignment', could be the line...another leap, there is a parallel/and diagonal with the dot nose line, and the arm and the head/extended linear visuals. So, another leaper. Descriptive, of TC. He is a 100% precision RV talent (select, or node or intersection or 5th dimensional hyper shifter, a Time Traveler ...travel is travel!)   weird, it means View Lord, ...like I said.   Suspended, like in a moment of Airs above the Ground, the royal Lipizzaner. Above the ground, I think it is in front of the eye on the ground in that outcome position in the lower right, but it is out front heading towards the right, the outer edge....that, as a descriptive read on the positioning, combined with the string of 'comets' or nukes like when Shoemaker-Levy hit Jupiter. Like that. Bet there is more too. Probably links to Valkyrie heavy. The Chariot papyrus. Heavy times. The last movie I went to was Harry Potter with my sister. I think it drove her nuts to sit beside me. I forget why. So, his hair blob is ....this shit gets weird even for me. It must mean something, that pattern, I doubt his hair is the 'message'. but, you know, they used it not just as a shape, but they actually have it as a guys hair.

 Easter Island's Rongo Rongo script, is much like the ancient un-translated script found in the Indus Valley over there. Only, the Easter Island script has a space inserted in each letterform. If you close the center gap you can see similar patterns to the letters. See? Easy to read old visuals. Just interface them onto likely links to reality. When you push an oar, you lean forward, in the direction you are traveling in, these little on the boats fringe people, are leaning towards up, the slant of the lines, the meaning of the triangle near to it, another determinative, to take into consideration the slant of the fringe people, (it is a slant triangle with the fringe people lines on it). Since this written rongorongo script bears similarities (without the center gap), to script form from the Indus Valley, it is in the same vicinity as the ancient languages of the Egyptians, some indication found here in these visuals, too. As well as the Elamite. Many ships, in their language View Theme. The belly carving on the Easter Island statue monoliths, likely reflecting this ranging East and West, by ship. There are glimpses of shared language roots, in the visuals. Easter Island is way out in the middle of nowhere. Maybe, it would take a pre-cog sensing to find this island in the deep space of ocean, like the Remote Views outwards in the ocean of space, to finding the planets. Precognitive psychics, clairvoyants and Viewers tune into things and then provide a Reading. That is why it is called consulting an Oracle. It is not a television, not an evil microwave, not sinister radio waves. Most of us know this already in 2008. Living in our free and open minded society and all. (looks alien or what eh?) there is a heart on the end. Maybe it is evidence of future time travelers!

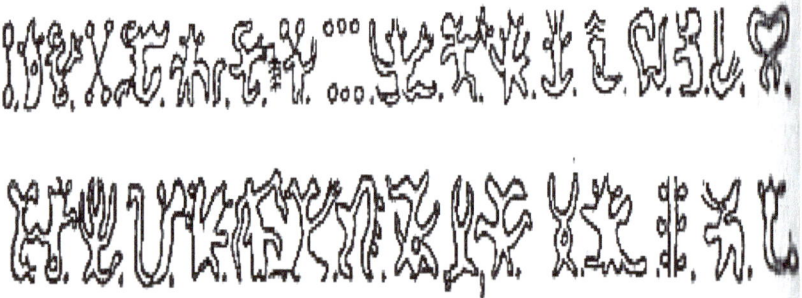
ancient Rongo Rongo script

'Easter Island' View 2006; Easter Island carved statues; RV visuals could match sub with men

At top, first letter of Rongo matches South Arabic, left, in this line of old script.

Rowing East; *Rongo Rongo* script excerpts; similar to other ancient language visuals, ie: Egyptian flag, reversed; Elamite ship letter form; ship with fringe people on it; flags

Views function as windows into difficulties, included. Sometimes clues may surface regarding an unknown matter. Usually, but not limited to, regarding security issues. In that regards, in terms of the visual descripton of the term or reference to the act of falling, it may not be so literal all the time. Sometimes, maybe falling is for follicle like a hair follicle, not really falling, just a thought. They're like hieroglyphs, they shift and get coloured in for meaning, and details, as they unravel. Yeah, it depends on what is around them. I hear shovel, I look for shovel. A starting or jump point. Otherwise, it just seems sometimes things surface, or perhaps another way of saying it would be the Veil lifting. More details coming to light, or simply a different time frame with more to make sense from. For following a trail linked by intuitive forces as much as any pointers. Women's intuition, like. Along with the empathy. And the psi, of course. As such, with the view's and the intuitions and feelings being so engraved, or developed, so familiar and all encompassing in terms of the planet and its occupants, the faces are everywhere, at times. Shifting, changing, like smoke, wispy visionary substance. Not that big a deal. But not all that useful as such, either. Too prolific. But, once you see something to link to, as a focus, and work around the vision area surrounding it, or the overall, maybe there is better chance of linking to something visually, that interprets into something useful. That said, I would not be surprised to find that it was the opposite of my impression. Like I said, this is lousy for any individual finding or rescue. However, when it is precise, it is, just that. Precise. Not to be entirely discounted or overlooked either. The value of 'wooden walls', and quintessential Oracles.

'Chariot' papyrus (enlarged) front dog's rear legs; straps in-between dots; leg straps

Looking at the Chariot View papyrus, notice in this enlargement, the front dog has straps on his leg. A match to the actual military outfit in our times. Providing an excellent visually descriptive link to our Time Context. Also he has the bad guy's head in his mouth at the front, in the lead. So even if we win in the outcome, doesn't mean it is going to be a walk in the park. Above the hand of the guy with the lead dog, above is a snake coming down and they are tied right at the tip in the very most far frontal position. Descriptive of a tie, like the election.

It is linking to this Time Context not only in an overall but limited time frame, but also to the Time of Now in the particular. It is a View of the current conflict. Here and over there. Again, they're all tied. They are all tied up under/alongside the horses. The little enemy guys the dogs have. You can see all the ties, lots of ropes and loops and swirls. And propeller blades too. Both water and air craft.

The View theme components include objects and links to visual reference to the other wars and conflicts of Earth. The visual wings on a pilot's uniform are very much like the wings of the hieroglyphic Views. Found in the corners of both the Chariot papyrus, and the 2nd Bow papyrus.

Saudi oil field; Chariot View reverse negative image horse legs (dots) match

In the photo of the oil field, note the curved lines, 2 sets of them, like the multi-legs of the horses in the Chariot View, only reversed, upside down, descriptive, and the curves, along the chariot base itself. From the overall air view down to particular indicators or markers, I think this fits enough to count as part of the View Theme linked to this Time Context.

The curly shape in the end of the tensioned reigns, is matched to the one in the symbol behind the Pope. Ancient roots and entanglement. This being the Muslim Holy War and Anti-Crusade(rs), current Time Context means this is extremely relevant.

A hitch, a knot, a *tie*, a tightener, a fastener, a prop, a propeller, it is land and sea and sky and space comprehensive. If you jump or teleport or however else, travel from one point to another point, and extending the concept to of course include jumps from one solar system to another. Heading for the stars. And with the old roots of the ancient Egyptian terror cult firmly trampled and restrained beneath the chariot of advanced understanding and the greater quest for the stars. And the vehicle to get us there. A worthwhile project in itself. I could spend forever and a day on this one painting alone, linking it to reveal the trail to stars.

Upper left quadrant, of the Chariot piece, is a lap top, open. As if looking at it from the side, with two lines of script inside it's form. The input and the output; the screen and the keyboard. The ability to form the hieroglyphs that is so cool. And it looks like they are visually describing solar power for the energy source.Extended into a View link with a Time Context relevant View Theme, from around 1981 or 82, a pen and ink with birds/tree entanglement. Like the conflict described by the old View Theme, under the horse.

And yes, always, it was a view of light at the end of the tunnel. And there is a light post and there is a Light in the forest and there is fluid motion. And there is not a single straight line in this painting. Well, one almost alluding to straightness, in the bow shaped curve, straight as an arrow.

Almost. I just know it would have a curved structure. I had this thing about no straight lines, desiring a fluid expression.

I can read, that is top and foremost on that ancient Egyptian papyrus. The Chariot. That circular disk is the Sun, they worshipped Ra. Ra was the natural clean energy of the Sun. the Compass Rose. The opposite is the oil. Oil and coal (unless they really do have Alchemy) are the wrong way, and the Sun and Solar and Wind, the Wings holding up the Sun. and if you can't read that. They didn't make oil and the sun. but that's what I am reading on this. As humans on Earth we get to go one way. We ditch the oil. Nuclear power plants would be a good intermediate step I guess. They need to get off the addiction and onto the only way to go. They need to meet up with the future for the children, starting now. You have to start out firmly heading in the right direction. You don't go charging off blindfolded in a Chariot. That does kinda look like a Pirate's hat though, eh? Maybe Space Pirates will come and eat the fat and make all the old young, my favourite. A long list. No wonder they don't want me yaking for them. I don't say things like, Aliens are making me say this, now do I? Hey maybe they are. I don't mind if they are, I agree with them. You can read it in the top left of the papyrus. Just kidding.Definitely a Sun for solar, and connects to the laptop join, getting computers seriously happening. The solar disks ride the chariot, the others are trampled below. The dark. The downtrodden and entangled masses. They should take heed and maybe stop their self terminating political and holy war antics and start thinking of how they are going to be dealing with an accelerating future and it is a mess. Unless you are firmly into Bin and the Stone Age Revival for all, they intend for us, you likely wouldn't find this too motivating. It is like being able to readily decode a stream of continual messages, all connecting at nexus points, that sure looks like lettering in scrobble land, running through that chariot piece too, at the bottom, all the long celtic looking interwoven lines in the tangle. (and no, you don't just go along and line up what I type religiously with what is on the tv or the media else where. They are corrupt. Not a reliable source of accuracy. Did you listen to that who was it Tokyo Rose for your information? That is what they have become. And you can take that to their bank. Oh, back to the papyrus. We use nuclear for clear energy, not murdering 'jewish pig dogs'. We need to get rid of those guys. Use bags. There is only one way to read that. That is the whole central theme of that papyrus. Aim for solar clean energy. Written all over this View Theme using the complex language of *TimeVision*.

Remote Viewing, with precognition is a form of Time Vision. With instructions. Highly visual, overlapping. Extremely precise and timely. Hence, the wizard, mer. These are not time lines they are Mer Lines. They transcend linear timelines. Merlin's Cross, an early symbol used by Christ. He used the symbol of the fish too. Shaped very much like the one on the rocks at Petra. Don't forget, Jesus himself was persecuted for 'Prophecy'. Mark 14- …"and some began to spit at Him and to blindfold Him and to beat Him with their fists and to say to Him 'Prophecy'. And the officers received Him with slaps in the face." They were clearly persecuting Christ for 'Prophecy'. There is no other understanding.

Ancient directions, pointing in the right direction for the survival of Earthlife. And, of course, like most View Themes, of some survival significance. Which it of course is. I still like solar and wind and other alternative sources.

Additionally, the Chariot papyrus links its View Theme to these current photos of the US Military in Arghandab, near Kabul in Afghanistan. Removing Taliban ghoul creatures who had invaded villages like modern vicious land pirates.

As ever, the View Themes are extremely precise. Hence the use of X for Xtreme flow using a familiar Stargate portal. Clearly these are visual links to the one and the same Time Context, as the solar and wind energy concerns. Note the marker of the tail of the ISAF helicopter, looking like a small windmill.

Enlarged loop from Chariot View; loop handle rope on side of arms brought into Iraq from Iran, for their demented murder campaign; hieroglyphs with loops.

  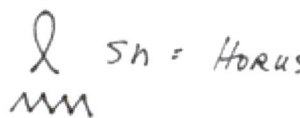

Pope Benedict XVI; similar loops behind; loop hieroglyph 'Horus'

    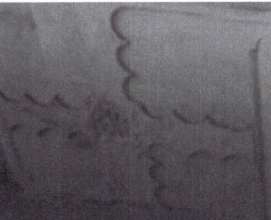

Australian mass; 'Book of Kells' cross; Chariot View cross; PRV cross; Rosslyn cross

Laptop(?) sci-tech 90 degrees, between large orbs; RV 1982; match colours Iraq, 2008

  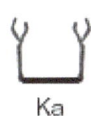

U.S. military troops in Afghanistan, 2008; ISAF helicopter, Kabul; Ka, immortal energy

In this last paint I can see it near the top, in brownish. It is more the feel to the thing at times. That is where it is like a heightened or what could be called an extra polishing say, of a sense. Most likely the empathy coming in as a way of giving an id to something. We recognize things on all levels and there is perhaps a psychic imprint. An empathically sensed signature for the reader to decipher. Like well worn ruts on a trail marking the frequented lanes.

These Views are best thought of as descriptive in content. We still do the human interpretation. Like any piece of art. In any creative form.

Looking at the following pictures, the first one is the chariot papyrus done as its negative by computer manipulations. The next are photos taken off-screen of the Nasa eva (spacewalks) showing the typical colors of space Views as actually experienced by the astronauts.

Following the same descriptive lines as the ancient Chariot done up as it's negative courtesy of the computer works software. Visually descriptive as a View Theme. It is the easily recognizable View Theme of the Arch and the Tangent. The archer taking aim at following a trail to the stars.

Connecting to the original oil painting set from 1983/84. Immediately following the intense intuited Views recorded here in Section Receptive. Since you have to be receptive to the forces of the creative. Basic 'I Ching', number one is the creative and number two is the receptive. Star travel requires a great deal of faith and an open mind.

I did notice, that behind at the church that Pope Benedict XVI was at, the thing on the wall, was an adaptation of the ancient Egyptian thing, I scanned it in, the two long twists of rope with the circle with the dot in it, for the Sun (same symbol used today for the Sun in Astrology and Astronomy).

Quite probably, since this was a natural ability, it is crucial for those heading for the stars to have finely tuned psychic abilities sensing the way forward. Especially in realms of complete discovery, where nothing is known and everything is new.

The psychic edge will most likely be the defining moment between accomplishment and annihilation. After all, you don't just go charging out into **Deepside**.

Some of the actors and other creative talent are already psychic. That is a given. I would imagine the military can relate to that. The need for an edge for survival. Likely why they understood to consult the Oracles in the first place.

Just looking at the wheel of the Chariot ancient papyrus, the Egyptian Pre-Cog View. They are like nuclear symbols, the three triangular wedge shapes showing as clear, the others filled in. And the plants under the bottom, like nuclear plants for facilities. (match to astrolabes found with sunken treasure ship off South Africa, by diamond mine geologists.) Maybe that was why my attention was drawn to the plants today…the attack on Karzai might have been an inside job, already planted ahead of time. I guess an am-bush is a type of plant, a bush. Not I am, but am and bush. Ambush. That's what they did to Karzai. They were ambushed. The enemy was already in position and waiting to attack. Turned out Pakistan's ISI, its intelligence was involved. Looks like mer was the shape of a highway overpass, too. The whole language is one big view theme. And in the Bible, there is just barely a day goes by, without a reference to a prophet, or prophecy. Right down to Jeremiah One instructions. That were helpful, to me, with the profusion of faces. It can be overwhelming, until you take it on faith, and it fades into insignificance. The fear of the unknown, having been dealt with.

Recently discovered astrolabes; match to Chariot View wheels; sunken treasure coins found with the astrolabes.

Remote View 1988; Chariot papyrus, computer negative image; ISS photo, match to negative

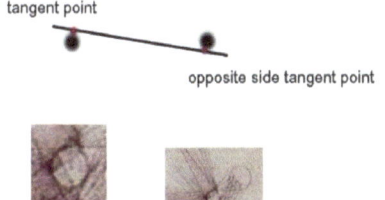

Tangents form the intersection and link points, for the hyper shift. As shown here in a drawing by Leonardo Da Vinci, exhibiting similar parallel diagonals

Back to discussing Views from a vantage point of **EarthSide** down to surface. Look, plumes of smoke from a volcano on Earth, from the Earth Observatory photo by Astronauts. (I usually think they are pretty keen when I see their photos. They take nice tourist photos.) and look how they are just like the plumes in that ancient Egyptian Pre-Cog View Theme, I happened upon. Must have been a Pre-Cog sensed tuning in and retrieval. A gem. I think it is endlessly fascinating. Especially the Time Context on this military Oracle View.

Photo looking down onto a volcano plume; Chariot negative image; oil well fires

Astronaut photos, http://eol.jsc.nasa.gov. Volcano smoke plume as seen from space to match with the plumes on the Chariot horses' head gear.
They already have an arrow pointing to the smoke plumes. Go online and compare, to see how the detail comes out in the computer negative image of the chariot as a visual match to the thin curved line and the small whitish dots of the volcano photos.

Pretty much cinches it the ancients had access to full range **Earthside** Remote Viewing ability. Probable, with the 5th D barrier breakthrough combined with a definite appreciation for RV. Maybe space and or time travellers were involved too.

Could be also the message of the knot symbolism showing in the Catholic modern day Church. There was one behind Pope Benedict XVI on his 81st birthday visit to the USA. The same shape connected to the Chariot in the View. They used priests in Egypt around their Oracles. Same everywhere, Delphi etc. it was never just entirely the Military. It was secret knowledge for the military and the priesthood were very much involved. So, the fishermen used knots. And Jesus was a fisher of men. His disciples were fishermen. They used knots to secure things in the otherwise fluid medium.

This timeframe *is* the Crusades Part 2 whether any of us want to play or not. So, of course the Pope is involved in the View Theme. If you listen to Pope Benedict XVIth, he has a great message for people.

Sending robots not humans into the stars would be sending no Spirit, no Soul. Just spiritless and Soulless constructions. A lack of true vision for the future of mankind in the stars. Not man, just machine. No value for the precious and the life enhancing.

RV circles, looping on itself. It is not a strictly linear process. Time is not linear direction only. Remote Viewing breaking through the restrictions imposed by time and c. Entering quantum facilitated inter-dimensional hyperspace. For tourist photos. Light bends, light has speed, speed is distance, distance is space. bent light is bent space is bent time. Like a bow with tension.

Connecting 3 arrow tip; similar triangle shape, extended and opened; Elamite ends/center

Or, like the tension in a taut bowstring. The sensitive dynamics at play in each View composition. The psi enabled, empathically directed and sensed impressions are captured with paint, as units of meaning. As per any painting, these are reflections or expressions of wave-packets of color and light manipulation.

Only with the enhanced psi energy directed to present spontaneous and at times extremely precise, Remote Views. Allowing us to catch the odd fleeting glimpse and sensations of else when and else where. Remote Views contain visual links to future matters which we unravel by following along with the descriptive storyline. Often, looking at these Views, to attempt to Read them and understand what they are sharing with us about the future it is linked to.

Like looking out a window, to the beyond. And then discerning by our foreknowledge, what it is that we are looking at. If every time you looked out a window there was something new and strange, it would be a bit like trying to read meaning into a Remote View. Indeed, like something that is before us in clear sight, in a painting, or explained in a written account, with definite foreknowledge contained in it, but still the meaning has to be *revealed*. Usually, our understanding of something depends on the links surrounding it. What else is happening, being the condition or state defining the relevant context unique to the time.

Meaning or message is revealed, either by figuring it out by connecting links and impressions, to form an overall comprehension of a View Theme, or by actually arriving at the future point, whereby the information wave-packet is then opened into our normal range of present time sensation. We know the future when we get to it, when following a time-linear trail. This Viewing method is very much a hyperspace shortcut. My psi directed Remote Viewing abilities can do an entire Mars View paint in under 5 minutes. That's pretty fast. Going inter-dimensional is very much like breaking the time and light barriers, combined. As though time and light are intimately entangled, pliable and fluid in nature. And easily experienced within our human range of sensations.

Also, there seems to be a repetitive effect built in, due to the pattern recognition, while resolving form and shape and color selection. RV confirmation and supporting links, make it clear this work implies at the very least, that superluminal motion is a real and achievable effect. Remote Viewing comes with an expectation of v>c during its performance. (See details of the Phoenix Lander Race in the book 'Remote Viewing: Knights of Mars' at www.nuts4mars.com, for real time psi v>c achievement visuals.)

Hence, bent c implies bent time. Like I said, gets you a Remote View Theme at the speed of Light. No sound or light show effects or anything. Just me, sitting here listening to music and zoning off to paint.

/Carrying along, then….If that was a view of a view of the window (Ethiopia) and including trying to describe the side window. It could be these are linked to the ever talkative old Egyptian View written so carefully on the papyrus I was so fortunate to obtain.

In the Chariot View wheel, there is a cross line, only it is running parallel to the horizontal and not perpendicular to it. Also, the negative space, the whitish triangles in the bottom triangle, they are the opposite of the black small corner triangles, in the window photo. And that strange single plant piece alongside the chariot wheel is Descriptive of the strip alongside, the partial visual of the side windows…sure makes sense. A Marker. What I call indicators. And the Lord sure uses this for/along with markers. I still don't have a thing on the coils of the garment. If the ark was in there, some form of angel's wings?

Pattern recognition with meaning. If you look at the rectangle in the chariot picture, the bright points that seem to form lines from dots. The joins in the window in the Ethiopian building, are probably soldered lead joins and you can really see them as like bright dots of overlap. Could be. Descriptive. And in terms of descriptive meaning. It would be the joining the bright spots of teaming could be like a joining. (in the chariot view, it also could be visually descriptive of the solar panels extending out into the blackness/darkness of space, very Time Context relevant. As per usual. Now, if that is true, maybe the Phoenix lander is somehow incorporated into the round wheel or some other part of the chariot view piece. Sure, that semi-circular blimp spot, could be an echo of the eye-patch I thought I could make out as a Pirate's eye patch, in the descriptive/story part of interpreting or Reading these Views. Deciphering their meanings from linking the visual connections with relevant issues and/or events. Using again, description and pattern recognition. And knowing how these Remote Views flip around. Their compass rose trip.

The ancient Egyptian word water sounds out like Moo and it is three wavy lines, (like the lines they use for Aquarius, or the single line, for 'n', or we. Three wavy lines, one above the over.) I don't find the ancient Egyptian culture all that sinister. They had equality with their females. The slavery issue is debatable, apparently.

The authors of modern books concerned with Egyptology, like Robert Bauval and Graham Hancock, talk of finding reference to time travel in their deciphering. Apparently they had to use precession to go back in time, to match the visuals of the ground, the Sphinx, facing to the stars of the same kind. The human faced lion of the Sphinx on the ground, Horus ON the horizon, lined up to its counterpart Leo the lion in the heavens, Horus IN the horizon (Hor Em Akhet). Describing time links. I believe and sense by virtue of my skill as a Pre-Cog Remote Viewer, that these ancient hieroglyphs were done using exceptional perception or what we call psychic Pre-Cog Remote Viewing skills, as well. Apparently another name for the Sphinx was Horakhti, or Horus of the Horizon, also the constellation Leo. Interestingly enough Horus (Heru) meant face.

Cern Atom smasher Large Haldron , '09 French Secret Service bust Nuclear Physicist (CERN) linked to Al Qaeda, N. Africa; as per current RV concerns of bombs, space and survival; Mayan face in center of circle is a visual pattern match to the Chariot's end 'nose'

Above is a curved semi circle which is typically considered to be visually representative of a loaf of risen bread according to standard interpretation without Viewing included for meanings. Leo in the sky could mean sky, since it was aligned to the sphinx, it was facing towards the constellation of Leo in the year 10,000 BC. It could be read as 'sky'. This shape, also links visually to our time, among similar patterns making up the shape of an aircraft's black box. Another indicator it also links RV to a match in terms of the underlying theme of survival instinct. And you can see that sometimes in a human's reaction during an emergency. To respond backwards. Perhaps a glitch of instinct, the compass rose effect interfering with thought and reason? Like when a rabbit will freeze motionless as a matter of instinctual response. But, that just leaves it easy pickings to harm. It is a counter intuitive or intuitive/instinctual reaction? Possibly. The difference between jumping in the right direction away from danger when it occurs, or mis-responding and reacting in the wrong direction. Could be that is just another real sign of the effects of being human in a 5th pervasive dimensionality. Just a thought. That just makes it that much more incredible that life with its built in death factor, thrives at all. So, it could easily as well also be reinforcing the notion that there is a correct usage for developing our senses to respond to the right and most successful way to survive. To lean in the right direction for life to continue. The Universe Exists is a very basic condition. Must be a strong sense to the rightness of it all. To exist, as a basic condition of all life and matter and energy. Existence. Matter over anti-matter, in terms of our Reality. Definitely something they will have to look into for any successful guarantee of outcome, crucial to any Quantum Teleport. That's one place you want 100% and 100% of the time. Or, you get like the old horror flick, 'The Fly' as a potential problem.

Of course, minus the understanding and inclusion of the *timelight* RV phenomena. As well, this curve can be seen as visually representing the dome of the sky/heavens, the Celestial Sphere, and the horizontal line of course representing the horizon. The lion presenting a link between the ground Sphinx and the Leo of the stars.

Perhaps in our collective consciousness, a View linking us to the modern contrivance, a face on Mars? Well, Cairo got its present name in 10th century ad from invading Arabs who called it el-Kahura, meaning Mars. The ancient Egyptians called Mars, 'Hor Dshr' literally, 'Horus the Red'. Could be the ancient Viewers tuning into the timely relevance of the psi Mars link! And in tomb inscriptions in Upper Egypt, Mars is also referred to as 'His name is Horakhti' and the 'eastern star'. The Sphinx gazes precisely due east and the Sphinx was likewise called 'Horakti'. So, you could say, the name of the Sphinx links to Mars. At the base of the Sphinx there is a stela, a stone tablet with letters carved into it. Written on it is the hieroglyph for 'Khaf'.

(June 26, 2008) The U.S. Military Special Ops got a super bad guy linked to the former nasty al Zarqawi, and his name was, -Khalaf. Close enough to count as a Time Context significant marker. The View Theme of Atlantis, with the compass rose effect of the black or bad forces opposite the good forces of light. Specifically for Atlantis connections, the bad being Hitler, of course, and the good being the American Edgar

Cayce back in the 1930s. The Atlantis beneath the Sphinx. The Sphinx is Hor Em Akhet, Horus IN the Horizon, the time tunnel shift described by the backwards flow of the planets through the constellations, formed by the astronomical precession of the equinoxes.

Time Context, being of utmost importance for forming the linking points. In order for the message that becomes revealed, to be accurately decoded and understood. The message content means the most in the time it comes into play. Like a soundtrack matching a video movie.

There was another significant message in this Time Context. The relevant View Theme was the grand delusion of Supremacy shared by both Islam for its Imam and Hitler for Atlantis. Madmen. So, considering this revelation, and Cayce made a point of distinguishing that the knowledge was IN the Sphinx, Not a tale of mad max, rather as per scrobbling, they are the main madmen. And they will take it to the max. The oil is definitely their new way to try to take us all out of their hair. That and the vote. They're like their aka wolves, and they are onto more than one weak spot. Spilling dinosaur blood.

Edgar Cayce predicted information concerning Atlantis was to be found at the **foot of the Sphinx.** Well, at the foundation of instructions (Chariot papyrus) as to how to follow an ancient Remote Viewer star trail, by markers, I found a time tunnel entrance.

Phenomenologically speaking. The movement, or the *foot, as the enabler of movement*, of the Sphinx. Both literally and figuratively speaking. At the foot of the sphinx, the name, the writings, most likely Remote View content. Whether done pre or after, doesn't really matter, the time View links running both ways, backwards and forwards. The Horus element, the condition of Time moving in equal and opposite directions. Each View Theme, with it's start and end, as able to be witnessed or observed by other Viewers, is defined in terms of its own Time Context. Setting of course, absolute limits, the 'freeze frame' part of a quantum correspondence. Anything that makes any reasonable and understandable sense, that is. Otherwise, you get not Time Vision, or future casting, but only random and chaotic results. Like an abstract painting, with no subsequent link to anything in the future. Certainly not a View Theme. Perhaps an emotional or thought provoking or pleasing aesthetically, piece. But they would be entirely without the additional levels of reading and meaning. They would not be found to link to things happening in any later time. Other than through the normal means of cause and effect. Like the reality we experience and observe on a strictly narrow and linear manner, in our usual mode of travelling through our one-dimensional slice of existence.

Capturing Views, enabled by quantum time shifts. Astounding discovery. And then imagine my delight upon finding the ancient Egyptians were accomplished masters of this Time Vision.

Another example of a direct reference to a time tunnel effect, in the following excerpt: "**All changes that have come and *are to come*, said Cayce, are shown there in the passages from the base to the top. Thus the real message of the Great Pyramid is in code.** "

Highly suggestive of a holographic process too, in implication. The concept that 'all' changes are reflected. Holography involves completeness, each point containing the code for the whole. I think this is possibly one way of seeing the individual wave packets as merging on quantum levels. More representative of knowledge as a contained rather then exclusive state. Very much like descriptive visuals empathically sensed as units of meaning. Reflection as sensation, involved in a multi-faceted View Theme where the dots, linear lines and curves, do link up. And often linking on several levels, at once. Like spinning multi mirrored balls, and we get to make out a glimpse here and a glimpse there, like speckles of star dustings. Empathically sensing enough to make a View Theme. And then the reader looking for enough points to form a cohesive unit and provide an understandable marker and/or clue. Linking to time, or simply substance, descriptively always. Link strength determined by spatiotemporal matching in order to create a Velcro like bonding mechanism. The cup, you dip to catch the flowing star glimpses. Or, they would all just go timeline right by you. Reinforcing the strength of the draw lines, by repeated pattern recognition.

A relevant glimpse into a few interesting Edgar Cayce predictions:
-"New developments in air & water travel are no surprise to the entity, as these were beginning development at that period."
"the records as to ways of constructing same (crystals) are in 3 places on earth, as it stands today, in the sunken portion of Atlantis or Poseidia, where a portion of the temples may be discovered under the slime of ages of sea water -is known as Bimini off the coast of Florida. And, **secondly, in the temple records that were in Egypt, where the entity acted later in cooperation with others towards preserving the records that came from the land where they had been kept**. Also thirdly,, the records that were carried to what is now Yucatan, In America, where these stones. (which they know so little about.) are now - during the last few months, being uncovered. "
-"the readings indicate that many of the people who fled the sinking Atlantis islands went to Egypt; others to the Pyreneas, or to Europe, Africa & even to the Americas.

"Perhaps it is in Egypt that the full story of Atlantis may be someday uncovered. For, said Cayce, copies of all the important documents and records dealing with the history of the lost continent and its civilization were taken to Egypt by fleeing Atlanteans, & were eventually placed in the Hall of Records, a small tomb or pyramid which lies between the right paw of the Sphinx and the Nile River. This enclosure also contains the bodies of many of the Atlanteans who brought these materials to Egypt, said Cayce, as well as a number of artefacts which will verify the former existence of Atlantis. There will be found, when the Hall of Records is uncovered, musical instruments. 'the hangings, the accoutrements for the altar in the temple of the day,' plagues and life seals, surgical instruments and medical compounds, gold and precious stones, linens. -'Poseidia will be among the 1st portions of Atlantis to rise again. Expect it in '68 - '69, not so far away."

-"According to Cayce there are many secrets still to be disclosed within the Great Pyramid of Gizeh, the oldest pyramid in Egypt and the one closest to the Nile. It is generally assumed to have been built around 2885 BC, **Cayce however stated it was built in the one hundred years between 10,490 to 10,390 BC**, and that the Sphinx was constructed around the same time."

(Same Time Context as Graham Hancock and Robert Bauval have for it.)-"As the monuments were being rebuilt in the plains of that now called the Pyramid of Gizeh, this entity built, laid the foundations. That is supervised same, figured out the geometrical position of same as in relation to those buildings as were put up of that connecting the Sphinx and the data concerning same may be **found in the vaults in the base of the Sphinx**. The entity was with that dynasty…when these buildings were begun. This laid out, base of Sphinx in channels and in the corner facing the Gizeh may be found that of the wording of how this was founded, giving the history…**information concerning the Sphinx, said Cayce, would be found "** *in* **the base of the left forearm, or leg, of the prostrate beast in the base of the foundation. Not in the underground channel - as was opened by the ruler many years, many centuries later, but** *in* **the real base,** or that as would be termed in the present as the corner stone. The info in Gizeh concerns not only pre-history Egypt, it covers the entire history of mankind from that time until the year 1998, which is, said Cayce "that period when there is to be the change in the earth's position and the return of the Great Initiate to that and other lands for the fulfillment of those prophecies depicted there. "

-"**All changes that occurred in the religious thought in the world are shown there, in the variations in which the passage thru same is reached, from the base to the top- or to the open tomb and the top. These changes are signified both by the layer and the color and the direction of turn.**"

-"Cayce referred to the Great Pyramids as the "Pyramid of Understanding". Built as a hall of initiation -through the process of levitation "by those universal laws and forces of nature which cause iron to float. Within the Great Pyramid, say the readings, is a record in stone of the history and development of man from the time of Ararat (the King) and Ra (the High Priest) to the end of the present earth cycle, 1998. Its records are written in the language of mathematics, geometry and astronomy, as well as in the kinds of stone used, with their symbolism. At the end of the cycle there is to be another change in the earth's position (generally taken to be a shift in the poles) and the return of the Great Initiate for the culmination of the prophecies. **All changes that have come and are to come, said Cayce, are shown there in the passages from the base to the top. Thus the real message of the Great Pyramid is in code.** The smaller pyramid, the Hall of Records still covered by sand, does contain a sealed room. The readings describe it as a vault sealed with the heavy metal and state that among other things, it **contains the prophecy** for the period from 1958 to 1998."

(between white dots) plant to matching plant, descriptive of Range; the legs for movement, like the significance of using delta as a marker for a mathematical shift in position

I heard the troops call the mask an *nbc* mask; they call a gas mask a nuclear, biological and chemical or nbc mask. There are showing here in this enlargement from the Chariot papyrus, two flowers or plants, with what looks like a standard hunting knife in the view range between the two plants. Inter-dimensional inter-linking Views. In between the two flowers. Like the two 'hands' near the front of the horse, under it. They use a goalpost theme for showing what is in-between. Just like I was doing by using the dots, to get your eye to make out the image in-between them, too. Knives would of course be something they would use, and their senses would recognize them as familiar objects. With well worn visual and language recognition links already developed. Something to click onto. Like a curved spacetime directing things. The natural tendency for interlinking or interlocking. A draw by form. And with all the heads, of course there would be accompanying weapons indicating. Marked within Time Context concerning the issues. Life and death issues, the ultimate in terms of survival priorities.

The mask, I indicated earlier, is also attached to a dotted line that curves around to form the shape of a boomerang. I used the font for **Australian Sunrise** for my structure and mirror of the word Merlin. Definitely, these are Time Context indicators marking this as a View Theme linked to this present.

Remote View white arch monument structure (outlined by white dots, far right)

Trying to find where to link the tip of the missile(?) aiming at the arch way, and looking for a suitable place to put a dot for a connection point to link to. Expanding the view range from where I had it with the arch foot at the bottom, to further along, it then showed a clear black dot. Running a line that links by positioning the computer graphics-line at the opposite sides of the two dots or orbs to be connected. The line being opposite and tangent as well. Meaning that it runs alongside one side of the one orb and the opposite side of the next orb or connecting dot you run it to. They mostly seem to be using this. It comes with the natural wave packet arrangement of the light and its resulting visual. The line formed by using the opposite and tangent method of connections, at the orbs themselves, then makes for a nice visual parallel, this time, with the foot or leg of the arch. (it being regarded in this particular instance as a structural arch. Specifically with the psi-sensed placement of the limits on the first snippet to explore in this time frame, now.

Attached to the mask curve shape, or descriptively the tight bend of the roadway with the white dotted line curving around on it, is a similar tight curve as the from above view of the map, over the region of Iran, specifically, Hormuz, the Persian Gulf. It has visual echoes of submarines surfacing, too, perhaps. So, given the other diver visuals, and the mask as an underwater mask, it could be waterways as well as roadways. Easily inclusive, and comprehensive as per usual. The Eye is always ON.

Within the area framed by this limited snip of the Chariot View, there is also apparent the descriptive visuals of a comet and its tail.

There was a movie, 'Deep Impact' last night. I thought maybe a faint echo of the 9 painting, the dragon in the sky. In the visual special effects they showed of the comet hitting the Earth. A Storyline? Picking up on a story? It is a 'within a limited frame or concept, that I see this. Maybe a story, like a book or movie is a story unit. I painted a small comet and dinosaur paint. But it could easily be an occurrence during the dinosaur days. The only other real comet links I have ever come across, where in crop circles. And it was the one that the Colin Andrews, author of the book, 'Crop Circles, Signs of Contact' put on his cover. The author must have felt a draw to use it up front.

Interestingly enough. And, the movie 'Signs' was starring Mel Gibson, was also about crop circles. They mention it in that book. More View links. Now, to crop circles. And the comet warning. Not sure I like that one. As you can see here in the photo of the relevant crop circle, there is a planet missing. An orbit, but no planet on it. Another odd orb providing a descriptive link to Merlin's View Theme. A strange orb having special meaning in Dan Brown's 'Da Vinci Code' piece of creative fictional sleuthing, as well.

And if Mel is again tagged as a View drawn selector by virtue of creative talent sensitivities, they that brings in 'Mad Max'. And in this Time Context with the present concerns about gas and oil, I would say that is a strong indication we could very well be in for it. An empty road? All these visuals of roads with dotted lines and no cars? Mad Max? And the comet, a disastrous tale or the tale of the solution. A comet, a moving star? Clean nuclear energy for moving our vehicles, our people? And as concerns our number one priority, I still Read this View Theme as saying we win in the final outcome.

 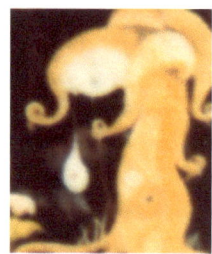 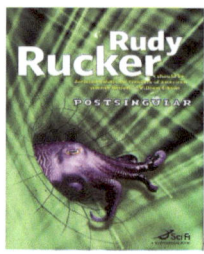

Chariot, blades between dots; tree old RV, plant left corner; RV tree curls match to tentacle curls

Inverted blades and a knife on the right, in-between the dots, within the two similar flower range markers. Reminds me of the flower on the ground in my old tree and eye painting. Sure enough you can see blades of grass sticking up, patterning.

Also, there is an online article about the U.S. Army starting its own air wing. The outgoing Air Force secretary , is named Wynne. That could be the opposite of my picking up on a win. The 'Coming and Going' old painting View I did in 1995, with the Air Force jets. Here is an excerpt involving palm fronds, from today's article:
"Army officers who are promoting the new concept have shown senior Pentagon officials classified video clips intended to advertise the service's increasing go-it-alone ability. One clip from a remotely piloted vehicle shows an insurgent using palm fronds to smooth dirt over a bomb he had buried late at night along a major convoy route. Moments later, he disappeared in 30-millimeter fire from an Apache that was alerted by the remotely piloted Army surveillance craft overhead."   The real eyes and ears of the war. So, the blades (of grass) may also link as descriptive of palm fronds. The cover of the Watterson book and the cover of the Andrews book, both surfacing in terms of a marker for the concept of 'to cover' today, too. Time Context, again. Also, the act of planting these road side bombs, is linked to the View theme of digging a pit, that

Watterson picked up on. All of these concerns and details are to do with the common ground and mainstay manner of the enemy attacks. They do indeed in this war, place a heavy reliance on the planting of roadside ied's and efp's, (improvised explosive devices, and explosively formed penetrators). Vehicles of hate, from Iran found in Iraq. They have taken many lives and left many victims. No wonder there are tears associated with this View Theme. A tear may also, be from a scrobbling description of 'adhere', thinking of the term 'gluons' involved at the quantum levels. There are layers and levels to this Viewing. Do I feel bad for helping? Most certainly not. Especially since they have been so successful in cutting the violence and mayhem down so drastically. Our English language is perfectly adaptable when it comes to meanings that are radically different. Cutting, can be a good thing.

I did cry for months and months, when I started this. Likely closer to a year. Lots. So, both maybe. I don't think you can maybe see this flower, I remember it more than I can make it out here. The feel to it. The form of the lines, like that. You get a cohesive sense impression to these.

'Chariot' View excerpts: Knight's visor (outlined with dots); 'Vanilla Sky', T. Cruise View of mask; visual descriptive, dots over row of troops/hats; hooded figure, snake eyes showing

You can make out a knight's medieval visor with eye slits. Descriptive of the visor visual found in the Chariot. More on the View Theme detail of masks showing in the Chariot. Follow along the dots to outline a knight's visor, and the small row of dots the eye slit. Another mask showing up here, is the 'Vanilla Sky' mask visual. On the end, the Zorro mask. Warriors' face shields and apparatus. Along with rows of fighters, their hats distinguishing them. Again, a basic truth to the description, as indeed there is a wide variety to the armies' style in hats.

S. Afghanistan, US Marines; 'djet' eternity

Combined with 'per' for house, 'djet' means dwelling place of eternity, here a match to the mound, the gun and the head gear visuals. Apt enough given the ramifications along with them. Considerations of consciousness and continuity, for life and death.

From the movie 'Three Kings', starring George Clooney, it is obvious that the 'Chariot' View Theme is linking to the time of the current conflict. Or, more precisely to a time previous to the hanging of their mad dictator Saddam. Ample connections. I will pull a few out and enlarge them alongside their matching visuals.

A match to the top left inverted A shape

Helicopter blade match

Visual match to the roll bars; A line of people in the desert is a match to the Chariot excerpt showing as ancient RV patterns for fringe on the horse, representative of its mane.

1.   2.   3.   4.
1. linear pattern recognition 2. descriptive hand attached 3. rows of bullets 4.View match

Watching 'Predator', starring Arnold Schwarzenegger. There is a hand attached to that one long row of bullets, and I didn't know what it meant. In the movie, I could see a line of bullets and then the guy's hand holding the gun, and his fingers seen from front on, looked a lot like the rows of bullets. A strong visual resemblance.

Another more current timeline, the Iraq conflict, linking the military operations to the Chariot View. A photo of a building structure, presenting the pattern of the fringe. Also, Along the wing of a navy Sea Harrier F/A2. You can see the row of white dashes. Similar to the edging along the horizontal outstretched wing of the two grand birds holding the orb at the top. More fringe detail, and in descriptive terms. The line extending out, backwards, but a marker.

fringe structure in Iraq; wing of US Navy plane; Chariot wing RV match

The row of lines connected to a hand shape; descriptive match, again a line out in the View theme, and possibly in compass rose effect, this could be not only a line out, but an out line, for meaning.

I found these common objects over in the Muslim Lands, in the movie the 'Three Kings' starring George Clooney. Set during the time of the US military operation 'Desert Storm' with Saddam still the dictator in Iraq. Obviously then, movement of the chariot and the horse are linked to this as an important View Theme during this Time Context. Presenting a main subject for our inspection. Furthermore, the horse's mane is people. Displaying the well being of the people under Saddam's harsh dictatorship, as the main concern of this View theme. With one smaller line, a child, at the beginning of the row of people. Clearly, the message being to put the children first. Pretty sure they meant in terms of security, not having them shoved in front as their shields, like Jihad does. From reading this papyrus and its links to the US and coalition forces who went in to help free them from the villain Saddam's block to progress.

'Vanilla Sky'-mask from 'Chariot' View, turned 90 degrees; match to the razor-wire at a terrorist female-bomb's scene of mass murder martyrdom.

The mane visual, descriptive of people walking in single file, fringe links to the flags at the White House *and* this razor wire, at the scene of a Muslim Terrorist's female-bomb. The compass rose as a concept involving opposites comes into play, again. You could tell from the full photo of the female-bomb's results, who is the good and who is the bad here. Obviously, the White House is not the bad guy. The terrorist female-bomb caused this death and destruction.

The reason this gets included is the mane-people were connected to the top of the one 'Zorro' mask. This 'Vanilla Sky' mask also has a similar View connection actually connected to it - the razor wire. Both visuals were revealed during the same Time Context. The Zorro mask is at a roughly 90 degree perpendicular to the mane-people. There is a cross bow or angular shape connected to this arrangement, that is divided into two, descriptive of a 45 degree angle. I saw it yesterday. The perpendicular I saw today. The female-bomb wearing an abayas. Not a good time for individual expression.

The theme within this excerpt from the Chariot View, matches to the ship at right, from the movie 'The New World' starring Colin Farrell, and Christopher Plummer. Also, a View match to the top of a nuclear clean-energy reactor stack. Marked out by connection dots along the top rim. There is also something at the top. An opening, with a star in-between (the solar disk, the sun is just a star). Oh, it leaps. I just saw a hyperspace leap, like my door. The right hand side snake-form, (on either side of the Orb at top), shifts visually to become a front visual perspective. By using the white connection dots at top for the shift perspective.

RV orb (top), with Nuke tower lines match to ship in movie 'New World'; reactor/rigging lines

I think the significance of the Orb is the generic rather than specific, to start, indication. Not just Solar? Solar and expanding beyond. Not just this star, our Sun, but also interstellar, one-dimensional markers. Likely more too.

See, at the bottom, of the Chariot itself, within it, the rows of lines and dots inside. I think it is descriptive of lines and dots, arranged, lined up to form the base. Delineating the base of another level, it appears. You connect and it leads to a new page in the View Theme. In terms of Reading, they add on more connective ideas and messages. From the movie '10,000 B.C.', the sabre teeth were also the surrounding area of the M on the Chariot horses' foreheads. And from the 'Last Crusade' with Harrison Ford. One part of the riddle was' only a leap from the lion's head'. Seems to fit with the forehead's sabre teeth present in the View. Leaping to the Orb at top was my next connection. A leap of faith. Camouflaged. Like the descriptive roots where the hero hid from the Predator's sight. And, like in the Last Crusade, where the leap of faith to get to the Grail, was camouflaged or Veiled to be hidden from sight, too.

The visual leap is easy to see, once the orbs of point connection were lit up (ie; my placement of the white dots at the connexion points).

You can see a descriptively anvil shape in my 'Mammoth' painting. And the large blocks or stones. Like in the movie. And the curls of the tips of my mammoth's tusks are not there. Descriptive of the tusks of the mammoths they were working in the movie. It seems to me, this View Theme links to the Chariot View, and is an indication they also

looked backwards in time. The tips of the ancient prehistoric cat's large teeth being the marker of this trail.

Entering into the times of the Pre-historic. Their gateway or entry point into that View Timeline. The fringe pattern, also meshes with an ancient prehistoric bone pattern, displayed a few times on the spear of the one hunter. Also, in the movie, 'Postman', with Kevin Costner, he says 'cry havoc and let slip the dogs of war'. Written by Shakespeare who covered most if not all of the old English territory. Within the View Theme, 'The Postman' written by David Brin, and picked up on by Kevin Costner's talent and also finely attuned View-abling psi, (like all the viewer Mars group and the other talents involved in View Themes linked by RV).

A descriptive scrobble match. Just because a Viewer picks up on something to include, doesn't mean that something is also a View. The Views seem to be limited, more like the wave-packets they reveal. Complete little packages, albeit complex within themselves. Think of it like the dark underlining of the Chariot View Theme, determining the area above it as one complete story, in itself. Like a story that we have to unfold or decode outwards, but compacts down to this one complete unit. You can link it to things in our Time Context, or other Times. But not to all time, everywhere, all the time. You would be talking about a state of all-colour. A white page and no info. Our world reality contains impulse, energy, sun, light, movement, progress, etc. people, things, emotion, you know, Life? We are just not a white or black, blank empty nothingness.

They were doing a lot of spear shaking. Visually speaking. Not literally. Interesting how it links to the time frame, perhaps. Visual markers. Like the movie '10,000 BC. Affording us visual reference markers, to time frame. Since they are showing and describing things from that time period, we will of course find any movie or article that deals with the same trime frame, to explain or reveal to us. It is not personal or Time Context specific. Only a broad and overall presentation. Many more connections. Lots to be found. But, purely by virtue of their occurring and being written about within their same time period.

It contains pre-historic markers that stand out in the movie, to View Themes about the same story time period. They link to the time, not to each other. They are not Views, they are stories and pictures that have some of the same things in them. That is all. You can not take a bone, and say this is the same bone. It is only a bone in a show and they had bones in that ancient time. A View will show bones. So will regular stories and paintings, etc. about that same time. There is nothing spooky in the slightest to this. Some things connect to a psychic window or clairvoyant, effect, and most things do not. You simply can not connect everything in our culture. It would be totally meaningless. But, with the highly sensitive and empathic guidance an Oracle provides, you can tune into these glimpses of insight. Useful or not. Like the 'wooden walls'. it is what you tune into yourself, in terms of making the right connections.
And just in case you needed more markers, I made out the pattern description of sails on boats, on the forehead. In the movie of that ancient Time Context, there were indeed sails of boats behind the sand dunes.

Looks like Merlin's signature M on the forefront of the horses in the Chariot. They look like the tops of sails, like sailboats. Definitely looks like a water picture …they also appear to be the tips of knives. Blades. Multi-descriptive.

1. View 1996 2. Stargate View 2006 3. Chariot excerpts- large M between dots, match to eye slit.

I actually didn't expect connections in '10,000 B.C.'. How foolish of me. Quantum 5th D land, I should have known. I just figured out their ancient usage of the lines in-between as marker point placement indicators. They look like that, too. The lines in the glass craftsmanship, show as cross lines, both using lead came as a wrap or the tiffany stained glass methodology, with copper foil replacing the old fashioned lead came.

Strange how the Viewers link up Views to where they need to go. I don't find this work thin at all, on the contrary it is extremely explicit. Both detailed and timely. A wonderful discovery. This is from one single papyrus with a complex View Theme I am decoding. They wrote extensively. There are likely many more that would be done by such intense talent as these Viewers. With many more relevant links, to this immediate Time Context, for sure. Truly, a glimpse into a forgotten Atlantean world of ancient wisdom. Mysterious and yet comprehensible, like landscape lit by a revealing moon. Come on, this is more than just a row of structure, the lintels are thin and a good descriptive match, given the Time Context. So, Iran is chomping at the bit. The long dark protrusion from the horse's mouth, a match to a dark form in the photo of the Navy plane, too. Another marker. They want to form a World Court to Punish the World Criminals. I would be one too! As a spy. All your security would be on their agenda. Anyone who helped in Iraq. Anyone. All of them. They want the court set up in time for the round of elections.

Bank Melli, Iran; Ancient military vehicles View, snip; tip under the nose of the navy plane; tip of horse's mouth, paint overrun like when spy secrets are leaked.

In the ancient Remote View of the military vehicles, there is a big bird on the semi circle. The bird stands for, M, em, merlin's signature, again. It means 'in' and/or 'over'. Perhaps the wizard Merlin links to this specific View. Here are some of the associated hieroglyphs that contribute to my reading it as such. The familiar from the arrangement for 'Sky' (with the determinative for sky distinguishing it or that as sky), the letter for PET, as already shown- sure looks like the media vulture sitting on a coin. You can see the coin, slipping down into the piggy bank, giving it some 3D circumstance. Rectangular ATM machines and lintel for teller?

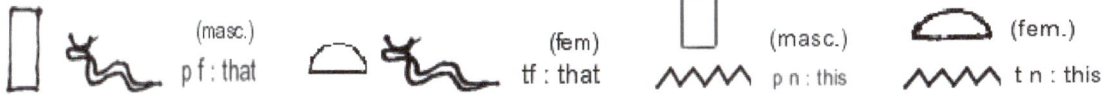

Hieroglyphs for travel, and journey with co-linked M/bird terms; note the View Range, between the two identical articles, defining the time dome, implicit visuals.

  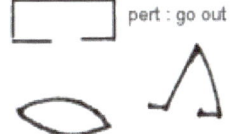 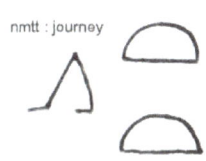

Abydos hieroglyphs excerpt; Egyptian glyph for 'per' meaning shelter; Pakistani covered high truck; View paint of cover swoop, like here used for covering the tops of military vehicles; View painting 2009; Egyptian hieroglyph 'see=neheh'; and alternate form in outcome position (lower right); in 2009 Iraq saw a few solar lamp posts in the spirit of modern progress.

View cover; cover; visual of a Teleport? Excerpt from Valley of the Kings, Ramses VI hieroglyphs.

Within our current Time Context's military concerns, combined with the surrounding hieroglyphs, it translates as the top general- 'Pet' for General Petraeus. Seems he got an official recognition for the win; with his name so carved here in stone.

The front of the top left corner chopper nose, looks like a foot, when it is framed in this portion, alongside the hieroglyphs for PET. In other words, a visual for extreme (it's a large foot), movement. Maybe descriptive of a time/leap. Achieved by performing a Remote View. Or is it more, a record of an actual physical teleport.

In ancient Egypt, there was an important distinction made between the Horus as IN the Horizon and the other as Horus **On** the Horizon. There is a fascinating tale relating to how they clearly held a perception of time travel. Explained in a book is called 'Message of the Sphinx' by Graham Hancock and Robert Bauval (page 216). About the 'Followers of Horus' in ancient Egyptian days and how they were urged to travel from Taurus to Leo. The precession of the Equinox runs backwards to how we normally know the sun signs. In the sky, the sun 's position shifts with the background stars of the constellations changing from Leo back to Taurus, not the usual manner of Taurus in May going into Leo in August. There is a time reversal between the astrological progression and the actual equinox precession. This reversal shows in these specific instructions, as they applied to take them perceptually at least, back to a time when the Sphinx lined up with the constellation of Leo, around 10,000 BC. As determined by a computer. Perceptually, and knowing as I do, the experience itself of RV, they quite likely meant something a lot more substantial than just a mere idea. And that is where you get the In and On as being relevant. One is on the ground, the Sphinx, and the other is the one in the sky as the star constellation. Of course, knowing that they had a visual Viewer takes that information to another realm entirely. It may have been a marker for something much more significant.

There is a papyrus selection in an older Reader's Digest, 'Unexplained Mysteries'. The chapter (page 207) they have this tucked into was actually about flying saucers. Time will tell. There is a tag on the end, the ancient Egyptian hieroglyph for 'luminous eternity'. The familiar sun symbol in the center looks like a visual reference to sun. Of course, including nuclear reactions. Sol is just a big star, and that's what they are. A sun is a positioned nuclear reaction. Send nuclear waste into the sun.

However, at the end of the writings, it is formed with the center, the sun, farther along the sightline. Extended outward. In other words, open, or ON. Like the on and off switch. The energy going beyond the barrier, the goal posts as determined by the previous twisted coils or wicks or rope. For length, measure, as well. And energy too. Like the structure of dna, it's twisted coils. Seems this is a natural life-form ability to going beyond time's linear quality.

That king one would be their Pharaoh, or the current cc, likely, the echo of the

American President Bush in the visual plant form shape, I would imagine. They seem to link to the main View Theme elements or components within a defined Time Context. A regular Jeremiah One, top directive for a Viewer to - See. That is like a bush or plant form on the left. The hieroglyph for 'nesew' likely is a scrobbled form of 'news', too. One made by and one destroyed by, likely. I was going to delete that, but Maat was the feather of Truth, and another Bible instruction on Viewing was to 'write the vision', plainly. With the feather of Truth, an Ostrich, and the current mode being Emu relevant. Searching Emu online, Wikipedia presents Emu Field with a monument marker that is the same shape as the Chariot View's wheel portion, radioactive patterns.

Emu Field; S. Australia nuke testing site, marker and match

Located in the desert of South Australia, it was the site of Operation Totem, the British test of nukes, in 1953. This obelisk marks the ground zero points. The article says you can still see vitrified sand and concentric blast rings. There is a visually descriptive marker for the marker, in the Chariot papyrus View. If you consider that there is only the one clear section of the wheel's divided portions. Rotated, it is indeed a close approximation, visually. The significance of the Orbs for solar energy, also denoting the significance of our nuclear times. Of course.

The visual went a step further and shows a P in the rectangular shape. I am assuming the open bottom is simply the allusion to, the hieroglyph per, meaning structure, abode, within, so, descriptive of being the one gone into the area, and also, come out again. Coming forth, per, with linked and associated legs or other indicators of movement. This is extremely precise in regards to the Viewed military craft all being related to movement. And of course I am likely missing things. They tend to reveal in time context and also just with new circumstances as time changes things. Different meanings at different times. It also say I I I, in this space/time defined area. And with a similar long thin line, like the ones forming into a portal or door shape, and the horizontal lintel is for 4, and the semi-circle above is visually descriptive of a D on its side, for 4 D, and the horizontal is also, at this perpendicular angle, also making an I, for ID. Wow. Time Tunnel ID. That must be what he got for winning the war. Or, another possibility is they develop Time Tunnel capability, and it was his ID. What do I know. No one tells me anything. I'm just reading it. According to the current Time Context. I think the row, is for the concept of inclusion of the troops and all involved. Too. Of course. But, they gave his name the show. A Seal. Must have approved. Star people, I guess.

Not to be ostrich blind, to the truth, there is left over, a tip of the nose of a helicopter and a blade is that what they call them? At the top. Terror, descriptive of terror. They gave the most useful vehicle? (Something, you would know) over Terror to the helicopters. Sounds good to me. I have no idea if that is even close to your understanding. I am just reading an ancient visual. It says 'Pet'. I can think of no other Pet involved in this war with quite the same distinction. And a helmet? Over the gun, as an (it shifts in how you can connect the semicirlce and the first line, not linear, more 3D. homage to the fallen. And guidance through the portal, to the beyond. Since two points form a trail. And the top of the first I connected to the center of the top horizontal, takes it into a depth perspective. The left bottom point of the semi-circle would connect on the top of the first I and the right hand side, of course, would connect to the center of the horizontal over the next pair of lines.

The sun on the horizon. Symbolic of taking light into the darkness. I'll bet they know the name of that helicopter and everything. Ok, IP for internet provider, that's what it is, the address. They always want the internet provider, your IP address, I think they say it. I don't really like all the fears Terror brings into this, either.

Attached to the lines, are what look here like triangles at the bottom of them, they are usually clearer, they are feet. It means movement, of course. To go forth from within structure by movement, is -per-. So far, I see the word hieroglyphs for per and pet and an em. Perpet, like to perpetuate. Carved in stone. To commemorate. Using Remote Viewing scrobbling technique, to presume some literal and some phonetic incorporated meanings. And the rows of feet, are the troops involved in the win, too. This is inclusive, not exclusive.

The feet one way on one end and another at the other end. Movement to and fro. Coming and going. Maybe it means covering an area. The semi-circle is the sign of a sun, on a horizon. Visually descriptive. It also was translated as meaning a loaf, of bread. Sustenance, in other words. Daily and routine necessary and natural rhythm. The passage of the sun in the sky, as the passage of time. In due time. And, of course, P for the People of Iraq. They are the ones who are going to benefit the most. Rows of crops for growth and prosperity. The market. Numbers. Plenty, for abundance. A double sun, double brightness. Ok, now I am just about tapped. It could be rows of tanks, or other vehicles too. They look so efficiently organized. Especially considering the overall military vehicle View Theme involved here.

 to observe

 present guide

I almost got that last night, the similar oil company name. I had a couple of the letters, from using it twice, but I didn't catch it. So I didn't make the connection accurately. I fringe sensed it. Like a net and it was outside the net, or not in right. I had the EM and I saw the horizontal lintel over the top of the tall rectangle, as being 'across' I got that from the Harrison Ford leap of faith, reinforced by the significant pointer, the Sabre Tooth and the Mammoth, being a link to Petra and the fish, and Jesus and the cross concept. I didn't do the PE by doubling (marker). They used the principle of doubling. In their visual View Themes, as well. Where ever there is a doubling, a message design is to be found by making the connections. Lines and dots, that is.

/ I figured out that the interest in ropes and knives is another lesson in the principle of duality. The ability to provide either help or distress, inherent in either. A lesson in opposites. The ancient Egyptian culture was very big on that one. And the ropes and knives, are a link to water ships. Like the tips of the sails, and the tips they had in that region during their time. This is a visual map back into their Window, their particular Time Link. And the concept of duality as their point cinch. I had to learn it, to read it. It reads like that. These are instructions you untwist and untwirl. I can see the ships in it clearer now, too. I was going to say I thought maybe they weren't picking up on or viewing the ships the same. But, no, I think they even Remote Viewed space ships. They were professionals. This is an extremely advanced skill set.

The fish hook and nets, another Christian symbol and water link. I think it is great. There seems to be some time essence or draw that pinpoints similar View Theme links. They can provide a way of unravelling extremely precise clues, in this Time Context, as well as its own, *and* its own Views, too.

/Like in the movie, 'The Last Crusade', there is a penalty for trying to turn the light into something bad. You have to choose wisely. When they try to direct it for their own nasty purposes, they are using it like you would practice Black Magic and that is not what this is for. They bring destruction with them. You have to be careful. Beware of darkness, without a light to guide the way.

Maybe you focus intensely on a point and like shooting an arrow, follow the trail, sensing markers along the trail. And the timeline you hook into, is the time tunnel. Where you can link to View Themes ahead and behind. Bringing into clearer focus, patterns of influence. Whatever gets carved like ruts, or grooves by being repeatedly used. Becoming discernable by the virtue of their being of a worn, or skilful character. Reading this Chariot papyrus visual, literally and from the angle of understanding and unravelling the Remote Viewing precision discovery that Time runs both ways. And we are able to tap into this for insight and guidance. I think it is talking to us about how to operate a real Star Door. How to get to interstellar space. I wonder if there are mentions of Aliens, warnings in here for centuries from now. The 'Followers' of the Hancock and

Bauval finding. Intriguing tidbits, maybe linked by myth, or signs. Like Mel Gibson's 'Signs'. don't know about the crop circles phenomenon, but it looks like there may be something more at work. Yes, like Time Travel and teleportation. By A quantum leap forward and we're already there. I am seeing some interesting things way back. I would not entirely rule out real corporeal time travelers. Like in 'Timeline'. I wouldn't say it wasn't.

See? There is a loop I made re-writing it. It senses the leap point ahead and repeats by linking to it, ahead. Sensing the upcoming, ahead and inserting it into the now. Comes out like a repeat, or a backwards echo. Weird. Forms, descriptively a circular or spherical unite sense. And along a time line or linear direction, by focus and aim, this extends or elongates out to form a tunnel shape. One way of looking at it. That maybe our lore and myth regarding these matters is actually derived from things having to do with a pre-knowledge of things to come. And leaving a trail of messages about it. Reads like a sci-fi novel. It is very real. Sci-fi now, I guess is the best description. I am taping 'the New Word', looks good. Spears and bones and shit. Great stuff. Knights' visors. Oh, they're Conquistadors. I'll turn it off, paint and watch it later. See what I catch out of it. I'll bet this twirls out like a net, a sense motion, and it is descriptive there too. /'Book of the Dead', page 29-

"...Ra it is in his rising in the horizon eastern of heaven (pet), **I am Yesterday, I know Tomorrow."**

Pattern recognition is part of our awareness facility. So that we are not rocks. Even the Rovers have this much so far as awareness capabilities. Motion, implies a trail, implies a follower. Not just existence, but enthusiasm. No, that describes human, still leaves out Phoenix, unless it went- look, Batman! Still, there is a point where human and robot are able to correspond together, as a reinforcement and extension of our abilities. The computer included of course. All gifts, life enablers, given to us by God. To enhance our stay on Planet Earth, by entering the enthralling elsewhere/when of the 5th-D.

I took tourist pictures of the links corresponding to my Remote Views. Here from the movie, '10,000 BC' you can see the first curved, sharp-looking thing in between the two similar flowers or other foliage, made clear. The thing I said was a knife, was actually better described as a *bone utility*. Makes sense, as they used bones in pre-historic times; an easy marker tagging a Time Context as ancient.

A lot of visual matches with things done by the truly ancient and also bordering on these prehistoric periods. Providing a means for identifying additional visuals, in terms of their culture, design, pattern. The more visual information you have, the more links your eyes and senses can pick up on. With the usual View Theme precision visuals, thus unveiled. Like the bone structure, and the huts. Many more descriptive visuals opened up now, from having seen their counterparts in the movie.

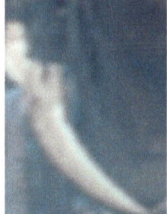   

Movie '10,000 B.C'; bone object match to the one found between the 2 plants, in dots; shelter tent match to descriptively tangled profusion under horses in Chariot RV

'Ice Queen' watercolour RV, 1972; modern day find of ancient Mastadon large curved bones

 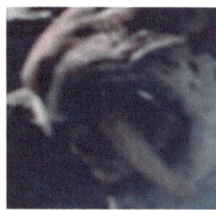

View match to Saber tooth (enlarged, right) streaks alongside it, as below between white dots

 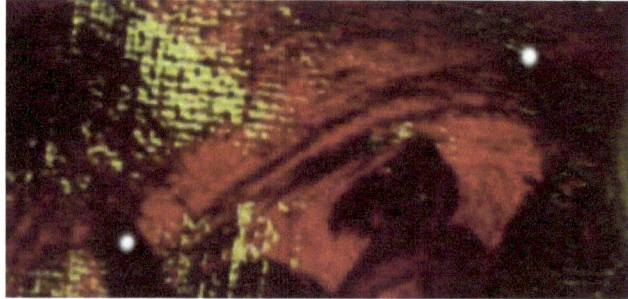

'10,000. BC' movie Saber Tooth prehistoric cat; View of matching Saber Tooth

Diagonal: feathers (Maat or Truth, for intent), lined up with the hand for aim and the eye, sight, far right bottom; Remote Viewing links, signifying a 5th-D Timeline

When you rotate the tail section by about 45 degrees, you get the shape of the hieroglyph for r, when you combine it with the wavy fluid line for water, or as a single line the n meaning -we-, you get r e n, and that means 'name' in ancient Egyptian hieroglyphs. So, as a determinative, the visual of the r alone, is to be understood as a mouth, not the eye, there is no inner circle or form. There is only the empty shape for mouth, and with the concept of mouth is sound. In recognition of the close relationship of aircraft and the sound barrier. The door way, being the central theme to the overall hieroglyphic tale. The 'tail'. the empty portion within the defined limiting shape visually presented by the two curved lines within the two point dots, enabling the connection. Both visually and in our understanding, our cognisance.   Aha! It was a name. (Luke) Sky Walker, character from the also Pre-Cog Remote View Theme movie 'Star Wars', with the Harrison Ford connection. (I knew it, I had the laser weapon on the side of the cover, eh) Humans created movies. Inspired by God, by depth of soul, including sensitivities, Remote Viewing included. (boogey-man hunters wasting time here). Watching Mel Gibson's movie, Mad Max, Beyond Thunderdome. Finding further View Themes. They are looking for -'morrow 'morrow- land; his name is *Captain Walker*, and they are covered in white ash. Seems to me the most obvious, the other markers are plentiful if not so significant. The 'cave art' again showing the rows of people on the top of the dunes in the desert. They go on to show them, in movie land, again as more than art. Descriptive, most likely of the reality of their significance. Like in the ancient papyrus, their mane=main position, being significant. For more information on the system see the book 'Star Script' at www.nuts4mars.com By connecting the intersection points and their respective parallel diagonals in terms of multi-layers or dimensions, follows along these mirrored and tangential means of visually replicating the precise and detailed hyper shift wave packets of coded messages. We get an outline of additional or extended meaning. Our present Time Context linking up to the View Theme. As well as other View times that linked in their time to the same View and its Theme content. Each with its own unique set of connections. With a View presenting overall concepts as well as particular and time related details. The system as it unfolded and applies so well here in providing more to read in these View Themes, appears to be hyper shift inherent. Like the necker cube itself presents the visual hyper shift by its very nature. Shifting visually between the 2nd D and the 4th D, rotation involving a space of time. Involved in the presentation of the 5th. The 5th D is linked to the 4th, and the 4th is displayed by Minkowski by a system using the 2nd D as its tool. That seems to be intimately linked to how we can trace back to understand the View's meaning, not just look at it like a visual. It truly is a Time Vision language. And like any language or mathematics there is a well defined system we can later retrace to follow along. It is there, and it works. No matter who is doing it. Just like any language, you just have to know it. Its' letters, or forms, its directions, up down left right, its' other considerations, if any. Then it is just a matter of applying it no matter when, to get it to reveal other meaningful packages of information. To use how we may.

   Here, taking the bow points, formed by the top left side of the ark lid visual and the opposite end of the bow's arch, having its first dot connecting to the end of the darkened and thickened portion of the bow curve alongside the hand steadying the tip. And then extending outwards both down and above those two dots in equal portions of visually similar distance or range.

    Here, using this Star System, of decoding, to determine where to place the dots, and then their opposites and range markers. Using opposites, range, double images, parallels, tangent positioning of lines at orb or dot points, and intersection lines and the like-stained-glass connecting lines between areas and articles and spaces and lines and dots, to link up and line up. Positioning according to the mirror sight lines and distance determinations. A mirror will reverse and present equal distance in its reflection. This is like providing the reflection with substance. Bringing illusion like a diagram, into a form it may be read for its original intent. Like a blueprint is just a 2-D diagram of an actual building structure form, either that is or is to be, but irregardless it is the concept that the blueprint provides a link to. And the concept would link to the structure. Not the diagram, it is only a go between. You don't have to insert the diagram all along the building. You merely follow its instructions, that we read or decode according to its patterning. Like the familiar blueprint it is only a form of visual language, it is not some spooky 5th D machine, and leaking reality holes! It is a Time Vision language we can read. You have to make the connections, to read what it is saying. Psi sensing is what presents in specific Time Context as to when and where to focus, what draws the eye, to begin and set parameters. Not a guaranteed anything, but a psi RV reading enabler.

/With all our modern advances there is still a need for the ability to successfully protect against the worst impulses arising between a man and an enemy. A need that requires their dedicated expertise together with the thrust of a fine cutting edge.

Having just watched the twirling of the guns and the flash of the knives on the ends, by the 3rd Infantry Regiment, the American Military's honour guard, at the yearly 'Twilight Tattoo'. I can see the guns' and knives' theme in the Chariot piece now. The hieroglyphs presenting as multi-faceted as ever, the gun in the lower left corner, is also a dog's 'tail', representing their 'tale'. Geraldo Rivera, (Fox Cable News) at the front.

Note the hand up at top right corner in the Chariot View frame at the left, a precision match to the left top corner of the photo of the men catching their rifles tossed into the air at the Twilight Tattoo; gun lengths in between dots; (below) RV of June 28, 2008

It does help to see it and then make the necessary corresponding visuals to see it in a View. The more you are familiar with something, the more you will of course already have developed strong pattern/sensual recognition lines to enable strong clear links.

Remote View of Military gun part Afghanistan 2009

'Mammoth' RV, 2001; '10,000 BC'; mammoths & horses, match to thicker center portion; Hurricane Ike unearthed a large mammoth tooth, match to thick striations

    That's a match. So, Graham Hancock and Robert Bauval and the rest of the 'we believe in 10,000 B.C. group', happened on some time event that is linking the Viewers to 10,000. B.C. I was looking for a spear tip, as a marker to use it also for horses, and I found one, a line in a circle, in between two at lower right dots over two line-people. A stick or stick person, began most likely with a single line. Hence we got our number one. A single line. The form a person makes in a single file, and that is descriptive and accurate within the pre-historic time frame. Truly a glimpse into a window on the past. The more concise the perimeter you set for a Theme, the more cohesive the tale you can discern. And establish as particularly relevant. The dots, placed above and beyond, so as not to obscure, (based on an uncertainty principle), to shape the window of the view focus. Like an outline to a complete wave packet, or an article within the packet. Remember the I Ching form and the ability to also pull out individual change lines, too.

    I'll bet this goes into the future. Using the other ancient View (tablet or whatever it is carved into), as a present Time Context indicator. That they were linking the View Themes to current times. Or, rather, that the View Themes themselves are linked to here. Time Vision language, linked like Velcro. We can read about it to View it. Cool effect. Timelight encoded. Using the masterful artistry of painting using a developed psi talent and being receptive. Using of course, at ultra-fine inter-dimensional levels, the principles of quantum chromo dynamics (visual/audio wave packets; timelight).

    I think how we define our reality flow, in order to make sense out of the brilligs we come across, is essential. Otherwise, we would need instruction books about everything to manage. Chaos and complexity would overwhelm us. We are quite suited to reading between the lines as placed by the dots. And it takes not just a psychic talent, maybe to open the door and light the route, but it is most likely something comprehensive to sentient creatures. Us included. The trail is an open route for all. But you have to be aiming in the right direction. If you're standing and fighting at the door, you're not traveling or moving forward, and that is not the route. You won't get anywhere. Petrified at the door, or embarking on a worthy journey. Heading off into the challenges of **Deepside** or rock bashing dinosaurs. Clear choice.

I think the visual significance of the lion body of the sphinx, is to turn our attention to the pattern on the missing part, the face of the lion (Leo, astro wise). Since Remote Viewing includes at times the use of a *negative* image, describing the shadow realm. One slight minor detail that comes with the Remote View compass rose kit. To turn the light or white into black and vice versa. Coloring things backwards. What is white comes out black. Also, at times, all colours, of an interior subject or object can be found sometimes as outside the otherwise-thus-colored-but-now-empty shape. You see a colorless shape, outlined, and surrounded by the colouring(s) now outside this shape, that would normally be inside the form. Not always, of course, but at times. When it does happen, you have to reverse the effect, yourself to make out what it means. Like using the enhance feature in photo software, to switch something into its 'negative' image, and then being able to reverse the effect as well. It also appears, when immersed in reading from a Remote Viewer point of view, to also indicate aerial perspective over deep plunges. The standard leap or jumper view from above. Pattern recognition, allowing for additional information regarding spatial coordinates, adding depth to sight range.

Expand your horizons by experiencing the 5th-D where illusion is constructive not just random chaotic uncontrolled fluffl. When you follow along, you find little highlights. Images that you can sense, view, and use. The ultimate treasure hunt.

I think the very talented and extremely creative movie and other audio/visual stars link to moments of 5th D often. Remote View themes seem to link to other material.

Including the talented into a rather exclusive group, in terms of psi-sensitive Viewing. //Now taking a look at another visual match and its RV significance, the top of the ship shape in the movie 'The New World'. Along with the obvious antler forms, suggested under and between the horses in the Chariot papyrus Time View.

Visuals characteristic of ropes and ladders present as visual markers surrounding them. More evidence of pattern recognition having its own draw, linking the View Themes from one Time Context's Viewers to another. Commonality. Also, with regards to the shapes, recognizable and familiar forms. Like seeing the cat lines in a rocky cliff side. And weaving meaning in a way intended to link to an already formalized, structured 5th D mapping system. Established in order for us to be able to link up to and understand the visual story they are telling us. The bottom of ancient pit diggings presently link to the RV, as also descriptive of an inverted cooling tower.

With the fixation on monolithic structuring of pre-historic and ancient historical times, this would be as highly familiar and relevant as bones, to their cultures visuals. If not for the carved Remote View tablet with the precise visuals of the air and other military craft, it would be easy to dismiss this as Past viewing only. However, with the set of givens this includes. It is more accurate to realize that it is part of the pattern recognition reinforcement allowing for empathy and reporting. So that the mind and senses, even or maybe particularly because they are in an extra sensitized state, are able to select the strongest to focus on, and don't present with completely open and unrecognizable mix of elements, to the point of being entirely useless. There has to be this way of filtering through and linking to the most familiarly recognized as important to survival and quality of such, a path forward. Or it would be just wind shifting patterns in the sand. With no connection, no meaning, no design. Just random and meaningless colors. A window into everything becomes nothing when it is without something to behold.

A cooking receptacle, like a cauldron was time period, like in the 'face' visual of the peaceful camp scene, with the roasting food on the spit. I think there were many significant finds, from movie land's attempt at visual authenticity.

The military mission to reinvent an opening to an oasis, the key being the civilian's desire for a peaceful civil society. Where it is good to be happy, not just smiling.

Just as visually described in the patch looking every bit like a face in its arrangement. Matching the scene of a serene village with the determinative for basic Spock, 'live long and prosper', the popular Ankh. Levels and dimensions of meaning and reading. And rather than the dark pit of distress, this is the life renewing fire pit, with cooking food showing good hunting. Projecting peace and plenty.

//Notes on Viewing Hurricane Gustav, USA 2008- 1. According to the results from my prediction regarding the hurricane Gustav, as shown by the following prediction using a map, and the resulting extremely close proximity of the actual path taken by Gustav the next day. Aug. 31, 2008(prediction)-Looking for where hurricane Gustav will hit. What I found was an older map, with the place Tchefuncte marked near New Orleans, closest I can see. So, it is a marker, maybe, to the area. Seems bang on. 2. Sept. 1, 2008 (result)-It came inland at Grand Isle, with weather up around the Tchefuncte area, being now on this modern map the Lake Pontchartrain area, and over to Bay St. Louis, Pass Christian, Long Beach and Gulfport…pretty *bang on*, like I said, my first impression, this one.

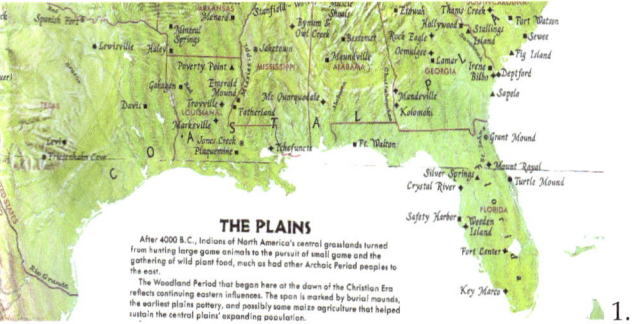

Excerpt from old map of southern States, pre Columbus.

New Orleans, hurricane Gustav hit at Grand Isle and went up through Houma

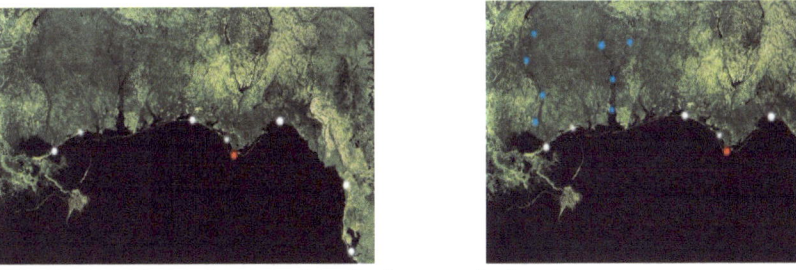

Chariot match to dots, under the horses (below)

Chariot, dots under horses match to map; lower right corner, x, y, z (right to left

A View can be very specific in terms of partial details. Or even precise, with a colour or emote, but it only goes so far. Like a photo limited to it's own inherent range and also the size of the photo paper it is printed on. Limits without and within. You are just not going to be able to see everything. If you did, it would necessarily imply that you were already there, in that future time-complete. All we can decently manage is a series of connections. Teleportation would involve more immediate completeness. Moving an entire wave packet from space/time/light suspension to a different arrangement in terms of its own quantum positioning or timelight data. Gps for timelight data, not just the regular coordinates, (x,y,z,t). Perfectly obvious, they were doing not the alphabet, it was a graph coordinate system, the x y and z under the horses in the Chariot View. Look how that matches up from an aerial view. When you look at it, you can see them as if they are all jumbled up in water, debris after the surge. It does aerial views of the plumes of volcanoes, and my Immersion painting picked up on the tsunami in Thailand, and/or Katrina, so, I could see the View Theme including it. Maybe I will take this opportunity to try to pin point an x …try some different combos, see if anything clicks, to learn from after…just humour me, as per usual. I am sure that is a View. There, I found an X, we'll have to see how close it is. See if I am reading their View message right in terms of this particular Time Context main event. prediction of where it will come in at the shore there, it will go across that area. How's that. For a landing zone. Time will tell.

There (in blue dots) is the x and y from the air, and the X is over, and up, from an aerial perspective. Could be. And the triangle for underneath, sure, they superimpose things, in the views. Lines up, marker wise.

Seems like the window is a match to this early view back at the start of this. Oh, and of course, the X marks the spot from yesterdays sensing. This was a troublesome whatever with the x marked on it, floating loose and potentially dangerous in the Lower 9th Ward, (where it was really bad at the Katrina hurricane, too); an army corp engineer (named Bill, see the View paint for Sept. 1/08 too), went in the water and fixed it. In regards to accuracy of prediction when I was trying to determine the place the hurricane would come onto the land (roughly), the first impression, without fussing over it, was the most accurate, if not downright precise as to the area that was affected. It was indeed a bang on hurricane hit. Interesting in giving due credit to this procedure, in terms of predictions of place. I had it first set as Tchefuncte, and it came in at Grand Isle, with storm damage around the same area as the former Tchefuncte, being up and to the right of New Orleans itself.

I think it was a pretty bang on for directions prediction, myself. That Tchefuncte good one. Described the main force, down to 2, not going further in…(the location of the word on the map, too, since you see, I have no idea how far that word extended as a marker. I don't need to. It was where it was.) good for a feel for how this works. I am glad the ancient papyrus provides a gleaning. Hence X marks the spot. It very probably did. You see, the X in a circle was the ancient Egyptian hieroglyph for place or city, or town, like that…a place marker. The gathering of people, the symbol of the cross. Very basic root human.

Not implying the X was any strange secret force, it is a natural enough pattern discernible in the Time Context surrounding the event Viewed. A fancy way of saying it was included in the message, of the original Chariot papyrus View, since it was there. Viewing is seeing and leaving markers, to be picked up on and linked to later. The understanding, of ie: the English language alphabet's letters x, y and z, are relevant to us, now. There is an understanding allowed for, when a view theme's message is designed. Like the selection of symbols of water and water related life forms and articles, for people on coasts specifically, in order for them to have the most connections necessary for understanding the content of the message. The connections are like that in that they relate to your life's experiences and tactile familiar sensations, your distinctly individual pre-conceived notions. The X showed as significant, and it sure marked a place alright, albeit in a round about manner. Perhaps it was the last destructive hurricane Katrina, striking almost to the day in 2005, hitting hard in this Lower 9th Ward area, that also was incorporated into the description involved in this event.

As well as the X symbolism it was literally a cross structure shape, like in the window showing in this Remote View painting from early 2006 of the flood and faith, with the window being also symbolic of the cross. With the gathering and hence sheltering of people, along with this specific daring and timely rescue. When a potentially disastrous floating propane tank was secured from damaging the levee. Presenting the best kind of emergency, the one that doesn't escalate. The quiet rescuers, the Army Corp of Engineers, during hurricane Gustav which hit at Grand Isle and went up to Baton Rouge. The Remote Views apparently covering this as an extreme weather event, worthy of warning.

However, given the nature of the extreme weather global conditions we can expect in these times, it could also be a much more over all View Theme concerning the entire lower North American continental hot zone. Too bad they couldn't get excess loads of water shifted to areas that are in the extreme opposite, a great drought region. Build oasis in the desert by transporting the huge water amounts. Capture the excess off the storm surges and whisk great volumes of water instantaneously. Great water teleports in the future, or something. Some weird and wonderful thing, probably beyond me. Hey, it could happen. Viewing is just a glimpse itself of a complex set of inter-dimensional occurrences. All entirely natural. Other than griping, like the dickens, there is not too much wrong in my little room life. Not that I think it is the way to do this, since I don't. But, in Time Context, the Muslim Men's Holy War, there is not much I can do to alter this fact at the moment. I am not glowing, or radiating or pulsating or anything. No strange midnight romps on brooms or accelerating parts of me or …nothing. Quite disappointing really. I am as normal as the card reader in every small town. I am nobody. I kind of like it that way. Oh, that was the other me, that was disappointed about the no special effects, effect. I make this up as I go along, it changes.

Following along the descriptive theme in the Chariot papyrus, of a larger under-horse outline parallel to smaller under-dog outline. In this case it turned out to be the Corpus Christi lines extending upwards, parallel to the Galveston lines (roadways). And another smaller set of parallels over to the left. Being Freeport and up alongside Galveston. From a view point above the earth, like a typical Remote View perspective, comparable to a parachute jumper looking down. It would be a Large Overview over the smaller under view. One way of looking at the outer larger range parallel lines (up from Corpus Christi and up from Galveston) echoed by the inner parallel lines with the smaller range of distance between them (up from Freeport and up from Galveston). Sept 10, 08

The trick is, you have to look for the connection points. Like with superluminal visual optical illusions. It is the connection points, the tangents line up. And you literally connect the dots. The system is clearly laid out, inherent in the visual field itself. Superimposition of levels or layers, one over another. When you are attempting to follow along and make accurate connections that will provide relevant detail concerning a security event, during a specific Time Context, there is a straightforward method to follow. It is the same one that I found all those years ago in 1983 and developed some sense of. I just never really had anything to apply it to, not like this. But, you still have to sense and follow along and make all the right connections. Like a jigsaw puzzle, it doesn't do itself. And you can miss pieces, that are right there in front visually. You have to get them to click into place. Odd, but a real system. I am not just arbitrarily placing dots. Psychic not psychotic. Heap bit difference. I am just learning, too as it goes along. I am not an instant expert, aside from how the old work seems to be lining up as well as it does. There is a lot of complexity here. I think it is a good pointer or map system. Just like a lot of the View Theme movies seem to go on about. Makes sense. The compass rose and with the multi-level effect, would be a mapping co-ordinate system. Like the heavens above, the celestial sphere.

So, the boat pattern I found last night in the Chariot View (at right, under horse) is showing because the nature of the view language is the ability of spot on precision links. And when you think of the place a storm comes ashore, that is what was there-boats. (looks like he is doing the limbo under the line…) I am just trying to see how I can fudge this one to fit…Post-Cog…anyway, the line is going over the dogs ankle. Do they call them ankles up there? Maybe for hind quarter? Maybe the dot to the right of the line is meant to be descriptive of -placed in the upper right quadrant? Looking on the map, I found an Ingram, inland, up in that direction, if you start ON Corpus Christi and run a line up, like that line here (only here it is seemingly, likely the View superimposed effect, as if it is lower down) if you take it up from Corpus Christi there is a place called Ingram. So, Ingram, right up like the angle of the line, only if you started ON Corpus Christie not further down... Well, maybe it is a range thing then, and it was the original Denton that I tuned into, Denton down to Galveston runs pretty parallel to this angle of Ingram to Corpus Christie. So, like goal posts, it is a Range being described...you can see the similar slant to the main (do you call them highways? We call them highways), roadways, at both places. You can really see it looking at a regular map of the States. Now maybe that is what the 2 is for. The two lines, running along the same slant, like that. A visual pair. Given everything else, it seems to fit. Like a piece of a puzzle, it just clicks in nicely there.

I forgot about my Jones Creek marker, and then I was looking around on that old map, and it has a Ft. Walton. Now, that would take it all the way across the whole lower coast there. But I don't see it. I think it is going in deeper inland not more spread out to do the whole thing like that. Mind you the visuals sure look like it when you just look at the weather-map clips. It is big but it isn't a 10 or anything.

You're not going to see the whole south wiped out by the one storm. It's not the whopper of all whoppers. And that could be why the View shows it as following along but the horse belly is the large area, the dog is like an inset, following along under it, that's how I am seeing it. //Well, you seem to have it figured as coming in around Galveston. I keep putting it down more southwest than that. Just doing the prediction thing and trying to fine tune. Get some map experience in.

So, if that is like a smaller parallel Inset? The dog shape under the larger horse shape, running roughly along the same lines, it could be that the farther to the left...

There is Nuevo Leon, for Leo and the Sphinx alignment (10,000 BC). That would be in Mexico . Now, since I earlier thought Denton, it could be the Range, in-between, if it is big enough for damage area, but storm effects into the Corpus Christi area too, maybe. You probably didn't need my figuring for that kind of range.

Visual map referencing; Hurricane Ike approaching following Gustav, Sept. 2008
Hurricane Ike came on shore at Galveston, and the Freeport area (parallels)

RV painting, 2006; Hurricane Gustav Sept. 1, 2008; Army Corp Engineer heroic rescue

Army Corps Engineers, hurricane Gustav; levee holding, note the white triangle area

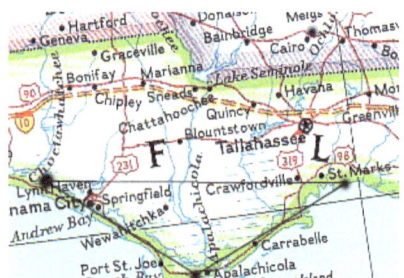

Map of area Hurricane Gustav Sept. 1, 2008

  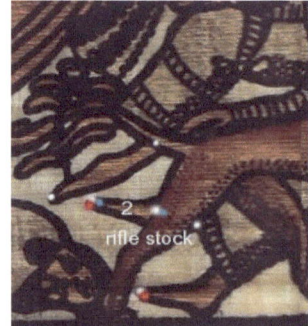

Matched to pyramid under the Chariot letters x, y, z; Anbar Sept. 1, 200

Predicting place for Hurricane Ike, in the southern Gulf, Sept 10, 2008 (11, 12...)

I will see what else develops…you never know, I might get another X marks the spot…when it gets closer I will try for it, the landing point. Well, looking at a map, there is the two larger lines running parallel and then closer to Galveston is another smaller like an inset parallel line running up from Freeport. Sounds like they think it is going in there. So, again the View Theme was descriptive in the way it presented its message or information wave packet.

In the following snip showing underneath the main horse in the Chariot View Theme, if you look at the mirror of the tent formed by the associated parallel diagonals formed by the linear structuring in between the red dots, connecting to the white dots, that tent…undercover. Spies, subterfuge, etc. lots to read there. The distinguishing of the red outline the large tent form under the horses belly. Between the red dots, are dark lines or guidelines. Looking at this visual from an overall point of view there is a larger picture shape formed. Looks like it outlines the form of an Ark, like Noah's Ark. Taking it right down to the bottom dark View Line. And following along with that theme, you can see a curved line in the lower left corner, like a crudely drawn seagull. And reversed, the same double curved line would double as waves. Opposite this, over the gap and at its diagonal, you can see the ark or large sea vessel from the air, view looking down. The arched structure within the white dots at the right in this particular view area. So, waves and water bird, they correspond. A gull is associated with the water. Looks like film, between the blue dots, and looks like a chain? Or chain reaction? In between the gold dots. There is plenty going on, considering it is under the cover of a dotted guidelines, helps to keep a limit for perspective, maybe. The main deal? Today, describing the Hotel? Could be. Seems likely. So, position indicators…the desert…those are to the left of the red dot lowest, left side. Those are dunes seen from above the earth views, like the astronaut photos of earth. And they connect to the red and the white dot. Seems like a traffic stop signal maybe. A stop and go? Oh the blue is there too. So, Americans. To stop Americans. That is the reason for the blast in the Hotel. To stop the tourists. Likely that too. No perhaps, definitely a lot of other meanings and connections. Might be an important turning point like the Two Towers and Pentagon and Plane Bombing they did before. Opposite...so, connecting to the lines I saw as ancient to mammoth days. This is that same terror cult. I already knew it. Desert tribes. Old traditions. Die hards.

They are trying to kick you all out and shut the door. Also, shutting the door to new ones coming in. you are invading and imposing on their culture. That's how they see it. The 'rising popular anger' players, that is. It looks like tunnels, too, not just air. But I see those as air ladders, ropes too. And that Somalia Yemen jihad area is probably super pissed off at your charging internationally, their guy in Sudan. That's gotta be good for some real angst, since they are so sure you all should be the Real Terrorists, and that they had the UN on their side, some of them. And the cable news networks, backing them visually, so, they are encouraged. Sponsored. like commercials used to sponsor things.

Looks like a lot of video loopage going on...me, I think there is a lot of Iran still written into the mix. This is not just Arab or Muslim as a distinction. I mean so far as trouble makers go. Not that Iran connects to the blast, but they are connected to the jihad, explaining why it is also in the View Theme.

Back to that diagonals, that thicker wobblied stick on the left, the dark lineage between the red dots? That is Bin laden and his walking stick. That is connected directly to that hotel blast. They are now focused on their Revenge at Home...that is their version of 9/11...only it was on 20/11...2 times the bang than normal? Who knows. It was 2000 lbs. so they are doing something there with numerology.

Mind you, within time *range*, they might have done it yesterday, so it would be burning nice for their celebration today. So that would be 21/11 and 21 is the mirror of their 12th or hidden imam. The Bible used 12 a lot. Maybe that was another mo figuring as a counter to the other religious view. It is possible. So, Islamabad. Might be some significance in their selection. The largest Hotel? Likely closes to where they hang out, too. They are like Iran, they move over land like crows. And they don't go any farther than they have to. Must be traditional in their bones…their customs. And the heat and water and the routes…survival issues. They are moved along in lines of routes, like going in between the guidelines. Or along the ridges of the tops of the dunes, a line going single file, describing survival procedures. Survival restrictions come into play. Sorry, I was thinking of them coming in from the desert. Tribes. I get bin connected to the fire, strong indications of spy involvement, and in the overall same time of this huge disastrous hotel fire in Pakistan.

Also with considerations in this time context, there are links to the ark. Perhaps to Ethiopia? That could be Africa and/or Iran; the Ark. The large theme, the flood. They have photos of the ark. Maybe they have photos that are going to come into play somehow for importance, that was a huge video-frame clip thing in the visual here.

It seems to help if you know what you are aiming for. I am following along the system as it was laid out to the best of my understanding, being visually immersed in Imagery, at the time, in the old work 01.2 that I did. It is a visual multilayered approach to making links and connections using the Remote Viewing pre-established mirror parameters of the quantum View field and its components. A truly 5th-D chessboard. I already know the language of structure, it's . Here, this is a written sheet I can now try to read using what could be considered at this point, an outer star link-language. Or, Time Vision. Star seeding in our natural humanity or merely Time Vision.

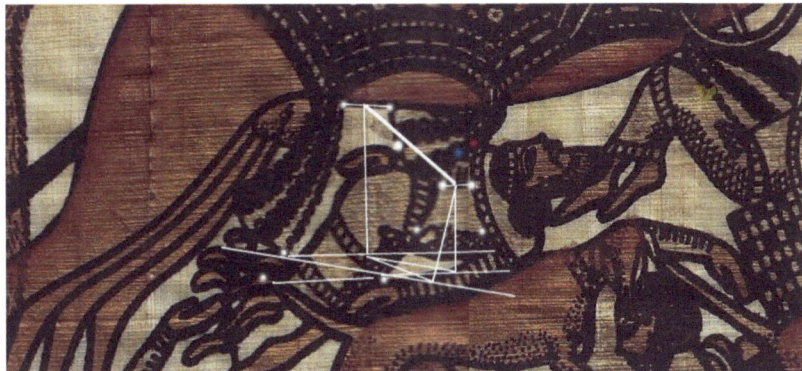

Quantum leap times, means we are likely on the verge of or make that already leapt forwards with the digital aid. I could not and would not be decoding this material, ancient Pre-Cog or not, without the assistance of this laptop. That one in the View Theme? And some of the writing I think they are making references to computers with, I think digital is *essential* for reading these pieces. RV details exquisitely advanced.

I guess Earthlings are children of the greater wonderful cosmos after all. This is not alien, this is Earth! Part of a vast network of advanced ultra sophisticated interstellar beings. I'll bet there are Star Ships here. Now I have to see them. Walking the Dog star, Sirius. It is a binary or two star system, lots of suns are, and that would fit with this revolving idea. So, the loci of the revolution of the ellipse described by two stars orbiting around each other might be also involved. Maybe common electricity and its connection to the nuclear cooling towers, as we can see the electrical outlet/plug visuals, above the tower on the right in 2D. You can just make out three dots for the three pronged plug (red dots), and the two strokes below and over to the left of it, a fork shape or electrical prong for plugging into a wall outlet (blue dots). As you just said, *energized*.

Ok, if you take those two tower-tops under the left of the underbelly of the horse, as one on the left and one not just below, but by a visual shift it is to the right of, (if you tilt the angle of the bottom base line the significance of the extra bold and widened for importance and emphasis comes into play. When you rotate the base line around sufficiently, as though you could take a plane segment and rotate it and everything attached to it, around so that the front becomes the back and the back becomes the front. The classic hyper shift visual dynamic.

Using dots to set parameters and outlines, and then connecting by tangents and center points, the fronts and the backs to enable a visual shift. Creating a means for perceiving leaps. If you already know what it is you want to get to leap, by isolating two forms. Just so long as there is enough of a gap area between them for the required parallel and diagonal lines to enable the leap at a visual swivel point. It requires a view field, not a length. You need to extend the usual two dimensions to bring in a third perspective, depth, and split the difference for they mirror process. To get a View to do a hyper shift and change directions., to their 180 degree opposites. No matter what angle you start at this is an incredibly fluid graph system. There is an inherent 360 degree rotational shift from the center point. A complete and unlimited View Range. But it is nonetheless still a predetermined and coordinated system. It may be the 5th, but there is still a Future *certain*. We do not come to any World's End point. It is this certain Future, that is relayed back, not the probability.

It isn't hard, you just have to know what follows, the steps involved. You learn it intuitively. There is a sensed draw to the direction most relevant in terms of its unfolding visuals. And I think I am just seeming to sense parts of puddles when there is an entire ocean in **DeepSide**.

I saw the angle of the camera shot is needed to cut the glare off the computer screen, and the online photo of the Petra Jordan rock carvings, is at an angle too. The angled over view. Looking at it I saw the underskirt on the horse, reversed, I thought like parachutes, then, like waves…

Could be wave packets…and large waves for a large Flood? Taking it into Iran (arks being found in the mountain tops, one in Iraq and the other I forget somewhere else over there.) the cia view is one of them. Aerial views. They were denoting the other landmark from space? A view theme marker? Like my jump rock? Just a thought.

I call it the Blue Rose, the Compass Rose Effect and the name of the Petra sandstone cliff carvings is **Rose Red City**. Fascinating. Could be for red shift and blue shift? In Cosmic terminology? Just a thought.

So, looking at the Views, the Viewer, is compass rose shifting, while the View subject itself, is doing it too. They appear to have different centers. The graph for x=sin to the third t, y=cos to the third t, for 0 less than or equal to t less than or equal to pi, is the same visual as the 'gull' the stick gull I saw in the last section under the horses belly. At the far left corner, that is.

/Gull shaped patterning, (also a match to the graph of x=sine cubed t)Like the 12 stones showing you the way to parting the waters for Israel. I can only show you RV steps. My math is lost. Mostly. Ok, now given that I had already sensed this to be the descriptive form or pattern for the standard stick gull in drawings. And associated it already with specifically the ark as an overall theme and the water waves, and the large hand waving in between the two hands. So, it is likely something to do with including the curve as I have found it here. Absolute as a mathematical consideration and especially the positive of the square root are definitely involve in an explanation of this hyper shift process.

It just looks complicated, all you do is go from center top to center bottom of each coolant tower similar shape structure. And then connect the centers, at the bottom, it extends, so you get a leap in the process. Now, the only part I don't understand what they were doing, was at the top of the smaller or lower coolant tower shape, where there are instruction lines allowing for the placement of dots that are shifted over, to make the arrangement behave with the required parallel and the diagonal in between them. That is where the 'fork' shape was, marking electricity or energy. Strange enough, but that is definitely a proper methodology for RV.

A pool ball for dirty pool? Resting on the bow. The other one is just on the open space or air or whatever. This one is on the bow…looks like a grinder or something…what do they call them? A lathe: a framework for supporting work. I am sure you have names for these things that are descriptively relevant. Those two orbs are roughly in the same *parallel diagonal* arrangement as the other two large Golden Orbs in this View.

So, www (well, close, the sign for 'n' the single wavy line, meaning 'we'), is past and \ \ \ \ is the future indicators or determinatives. Sort of. They might mark the Time frame. The present doesn't have the 'r' for 'mouth', just the past and the future ones have the empty curved area, that means 'mouth' in them. It must mean their meaning. What they 'communicate'. The testimony, since they are not actual but are determined by how they are recorded and understood (audio and/or visual)or interpreted.

Gull shaped pattern; 'Ka' visual looks like electrical prongs; digital 0 & 1; cooking pot reversed is a coin top; ancient cooking pot

The long slender rectangle (descriptive of area and below/above, like the sand dunes, to make the distinction with something so all pervasively similar in the surroundings, I would imagine), when it has the 3 circles under it, it means dedication, phonetically, it is 'mnw' or menew. Reversed, and scrobbled, that is wemen or women. The long slender rectangle, itself, without the fringe people on it, the people walking along on the top of the dunes visual, is phonetically 'sh' and the small snake is actually an 'f'. and 3 just straight circles are grains of sand, minerals. RV contains macro and micro. Other planets? that's what I am thinking, the circle with the dot inside is the Sun symbol, then and now. Other suns? The Net of the Galaxy/and/or Universe? Many other suns. Also descriptive of nuclear energy.

The overall shape must mean something, to the covering. You can see a tower rising up like the cn tower in Toronto, Seattle, and Niagara Falls has one too. Where you go up in the space needle to view the surroundings, have dinner, play tourist. Looks like the cylinder type buildings a bit too. The ones that look like thermoses. The top rounds also look like a lock, you know like on a private Safe or a padlock.

The tall structure (looking at it from an angle, so that it would have depth as well and visually show a tower going upwards from the ground below. Looking at it from that perspective, you can see that it is placed on a 'highway' below…it looks a bit like a ladder, too. The ideation of something extending upwards, incorporated in the view itself. They do that, they seem to teach and mention it, too. So, maybe it is like an oil pump too? Or those derrick things maybe. Oil, and roads and infrastructure. The Global specific of the visual for the View, and closer up, a close resemblance to a modern security camera eye. Just the curve of the wave form, matches the curve of the globe of the earth. Like the 'Da Vinci Code' where the globes or mysterious orbs are celestial. Like the ancient Oracle at Delphi distinguishing 'Wooden Walls' as a main prediction, this modern RV Oracle's Outcome as determined by Reading this ancient Egyptian RV precise Time Vision encoding would have to be: 'Water(y) World'. Here but else when?

Ancient Links & Future Trails   First Viewer 5th D   81

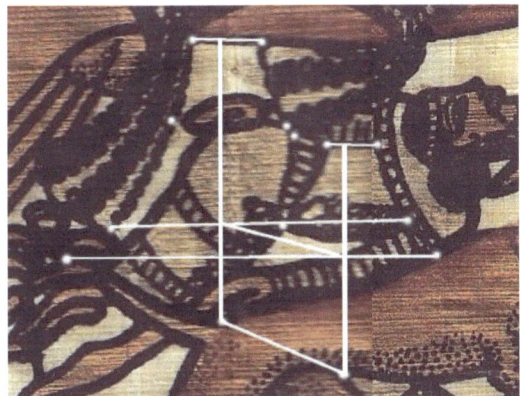

Quantum Leap- Connecting the dots, forming lines according to the system in 'Star Script' results in RV visual descriptive of a Hypershift Leap as the front revolves around to become back

(between dots) RV long 'tower' shape rising up at an angle over a highway below, presenting a visual of conceptual 3D.

End Reading of RV visuals, Sept 26, 2008; eye in dots at left, using *parallel/diagonal*

RV links to the similar eye found at the far bottom right corner; with upwards marker extensions, a precise visual match to 'WaterWorld' movie, with Kevin Costner boats and horizon. www.peterlanger.com
(below) 1. slanted visuals of the Petra, Jordan 'Raiders of the Lost Ark' treasury, RV carving; 2. Rosslyn Chapel cross orbs from www.panoramas.dk/da-vinci-code/rosslyn-chapel.html

 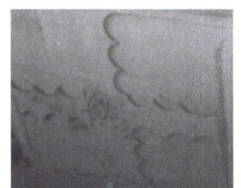
1.   2.

More of the orb and/or reversed-waves shapes edging the cover; modern security camera 'eye'; similar to the Chariot snip beside it, as a combination-lock on a safe; Earth match; Snip showing multi-layered effect; linking dots by psi-sense, following the system devised in 01.2, an earlier look at multi-dimensional hyper shift.

    They do seem to spread out as parts, or components to a view, at times. It is like this, when you're following along, and looking at it, partially or not, this is often what they do visually. But not the only thing, just a glimpse of a repeat pattern I am noticing, too. They shift (in any direction), going over a bit and then looking up a bit, you will find parts to superimpose together. Allowing you to connect the dots to form parts that link together. As if for example, you took a regular bullseye with three concentric rings apart and placed it on three separate vertical layers with one ring on each successive layer. Then, viewing from another angle, you can collapse the view onto a common plane, to visualize all the components together and interpret what it is they are describing. If the article or component of the RV includes any precognitive information, a wave packet with future info, it obviously at some point links with the time ahead. With the usual necker shift this becomes apparent as time going backwards not just forwards. Breaking beyond the barriers limiting the visual to the 4th circumstance and its distinctly linear approach to the experience of time. Enabling a reversal of linear time, by immersing in timelight and involving the 5th-D. Below, A is the visual leap of over and up, and B is formed by extending the lines. Heading into necker territory.
    Not that this is the only thing involved. Like I mentioned, since there are of course

the complete comprehensive view articles, the RV gems that appear at times too. Or a part of something so clear it is immediately recognizable with no other surrounding dot or linear psi links needed.

As well as using *tangents* as connection markers, the RV articles emerge when made out by interconnecting lines, at *intersections*. Just like in stained glass. They follow along connecting at the intersections. Whether it is three or four lines coming together at a point. The connecting lines are then placed in-between the dots that are formed by these intersection link points. Another level becomes apparent. Seen when it reveals its then outlined or structured, what. Enabling you to then follow along and decipher it if possible, linking to surrounding events and circumstances. I think it might be like a star code. Perhaps. Maybe just a natural timelight effect to learn from. Comes with the kit, from Viewing wave-packets, that is. Like periods forming a limit, a sentence.

There are several components used to find the theme in among the multitude of codes in a Remote View. The Chariot papyrus is extremely sophisticated and requires some advanced understanding to follow along, albeit the method or system of reading hypershit info packets is rather simplistic itself. Especially and perhaps only sufficiently rendered with the aid of computer precision to detect. It rapidly becomes obvious that these particular RVs follow with the digital persuasion in means and results. Meaning, it takes a computer for ease and accuracy in placing the dots and lines. Also, along with the psi for timing, such as where to start your points and at the end, where to limit the structure. Like a card reading. You don't read 'everything' you formulate within structure. It has to have meaning. You don't merely say, you will be alive and then you won't. You have to focus to provide relevance. Make that psi, intuition, intuitive-logic, sensitive to the SpaceTimeLight phenomenon of the 5th D. Basic C. Necker Cube (end).

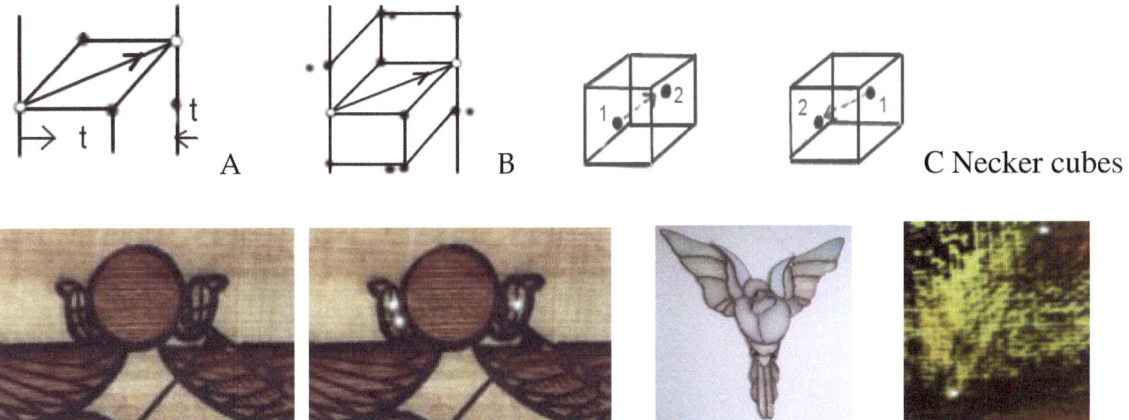

Chariot papyrus RV snip, showing a set of intersection points for dot placement during its specific time-link; Stained Glass Tiffany similar style lines; RV knife in between white dots

Look for intersection points to place dots at, very much like you see in a Tiffany Stained Glass piece, where the individual pieces have (copper foil) lead lines in-between pieces. Dot placement intersection points, with an oversight view of intending to form parallel or diagonals, or angular connections, end points and anything else relevant to the system of dot and line placement designed to present formalized wave packets of pertinent information. A Vision Language presents a descriptive View Theme. Note, this is not to be confused with the outlining of a cohesive view article such as a knife, that I pull out from a Remote View and place arbitrary dots around. This is an advanced hyper-structure time linked message sheet. Structured along clear guiding lines. Simply enough, to follow along, with a bit of persistence and knowing what it is you are looking for, within the guiding system. Dots to dots, at intersections, lines to drop down vertically, easy with computer facilitation; same for the verticals. Remote View Theme, formed in regards to dots/circles/orbs/diagonals/parallels (see 'Star Script')

Remote View October 12th, 2009

Ancient Links & Future Trails — First Viewer 5th D

The system, the Imagery tools derived from this Stargate experience along with the former 'Star Script' work back in 1983, determining a form or method to follow along. Like non-linear steps, a bit like looking at an Escher drawing that twists and turns through multi dimensions using perspective and angles, rotation and illusion. The system presents a few particular means of treatments, such as tangents, opposites, parallels and their connecting diagonal, etc. Means that you can combine and superimpose, frame and replicate. In order to determine where to place the dots and their linear or curved associated lines. The ones that when placed will describe something of meaning to you, within the time you see it, concerning surrounding events.   Used to manipulate lines using a computer for complete rotation and ease of placement. With of course the required precision. The guarantee, I would imagine, that only an advanced civilization, can decipher their encoding ability. This is indeed a star code encompassing art and science, psi and faith, intuition and logic. No artist alone, without science would unravel this. The quantum 5th hyper shift and time light are physical and reproduce with digitally measurable qualities. Star entities are embracing this guidance system.

   The order of the dot connections was #1, an elliptical shape visually describing an 'eye' on the ground (lower right bottom corner). Describing as a manner of selecting a meaningful starting point, and with two, a Range. In order to explore a certain defined and as set, limited Range to examine the Remote View within. Here, in particular, being the entire Chariot overview, looking for the specific Outcome. Usually finding that the ancient remote views showing in language script, tends to place the Outcome or Result in the lower right bottom corner. From my Reading along with the Views as they unfold, and they seem to be fairly consistent. If the script contains Pre-Cog Remote view content, the lower right corner end point contains the glyphs that relate to the main priority, the Reason and Resolution.

    In this particular Remote View it appears that the lower left corner (the far left vertical linear/point along the repetitive or mirrored parallels/diagonals structure that started with the eye in far right bottom corner) *also* finishes with some anticipation of the overall View Theme. There is a constructed link between the beginning of the motion, at the point of t=0, the end of the wheel at the left and the opposite end point at the right on the bottom line, derived by the hyper shift method (inherent in the description here of method). And the other end of the encapsulated timelight message. It would not be entirely inconceivable that this includes mention, of far ranging concepts as well as any that I can make out according to our times. It could be telling tales about the coming of teleportation. Instantaneous hyper shift. From here at the back to the front, achieved in a completed and definable form involving quantum motion accessing the 5th. Perhaps describing another leap to come. Comparing it or connecting it to locomotive actuality; like man's leap from living horses to iron horses. With the long linear diagonal extension that reaches out to perpendicular markers along the tangent point at the left of the upper most Orb. The next intergalactic leap outwards. The framework at the bottom, is also rather reminiscent of the base work beneath the Shuttle where it blasts off for Nasa to the ISS above Earth. The Views do tend to be inclusive, especially with structural patterning. There is likely tons more for meaning. I am a visual artist/precog Viewer, not a functioning mathematician. I can only recognize the barest of what they are describing. I see ice berg tips, you have to define your own bergs.

The end points, in terms of looking at a line to cross over at the finish of a race, signifying a Win. In this present Time Context that would be the reasonable outcome of this conflict. As it is currently being defined, on many levels of participation.

This first dot at the far right tip, leading up to the fore hoof of the horse, the tip at the front here also, for dot #2.

Then sighting at the tensile point at the edge of the Orb (The tensile point being at the tangent point #3, where the visual looks like a hand gripping a tightly held back elastic). Then, drop *computer-enabled precision verticals* down from #2 and #3 to present parallels, to the diagonal formed by the line #1-#3.

You can see at this stage, a couple of parallel lines (the shift from point #1 to #4, and not shown but implied, a shift from line #3-#1 to #3-#4), presenting a diagonal. Now, looking to form the diagonal's match, a line running parallel to the diagonal line, (in a mirror a diagonal forms the Reverse diagonal, the line and the mirrored line, combined would be an X, describing a place marker). And sighting up to the orb, like the line #1-#3, only the higher Orb this time. Finding intersection markings, the X clearly showing in the snake forms alongside the large Orb at top left of the papyrus. Once the dots are put in, you can see a tale of snake eyes. Continuing, connecting dot #5 up to form a diagonal at #6. Again, drop down a vertical from point #7, the intersection point of the *computer horizontal* out from #3 to #11, and the diagonal from #5-#6.

Extending the computer line, as you start it at the point #5 and holding the line, curve it up and see visually, if there is anything that leaps out to you as a potential connection point. The computer holds the line as you arc it around, the same as a basic old fashioned ruler or measuring stick that holds its shape as you push it along over a paper, making a sweeping arc shape. Like that. Nothing too mysterious. When you are arcing the extended line around, you can see the intersection points on the snake alongside the Orb, aligning up with the same diagonal form. It connects, dot to dot forming the line #5-#6.

Notice how accurately the horizontal covers the lower horizontal of the laptop form in the papyrus View Theme. Taking it from the tensile point at the perpendicular tangent of the Orb, lower level, extending a horizontal line to the end point of the view, and beyond as line #3-11.

Again, another line parallel to this horizontal, running along as the line formed by the dots #2-#12. Then shifting from the point #9 down to #13, and forming a line from point #8 to #9, as a parallel to the line already formed from the large top Orb to the base down vertical from the horse's mane, being a line formed by #6 -#7- #8. You can now see a very sharp angle formed by #9 down to #8 and then up to #13. Very similar to the tensile sharp angle formed by dark lines already occurring (from the base of the back loop on the Chariot to the back of the lower Orb) in the papyrus View Theme. And, again to finish off, a final vertical computer drop down from #13. Appropriately enough, this new intersection position at the base of the View, now describes the point where it is the wheel moving forward, and the past is left behind the wheel structure as it rests here, on the ground.

 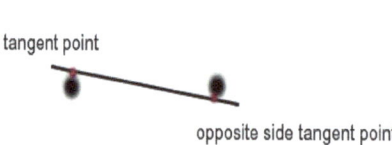 

Dot and line placement showing an example of using opposite tangent points; the amazing Oracle 'I Ching' window, showing parallel legs (lines) diagonal across lines as visual descriptives, as per typical RV. See 'Star Script' by 1st 5th for more details on the Quantum 5th D Hypershift Psi Leaps; A) Parallel Diagonal & Perpendicular

A)

Ancient Links & Future Trails   First Viewer 5th D   89

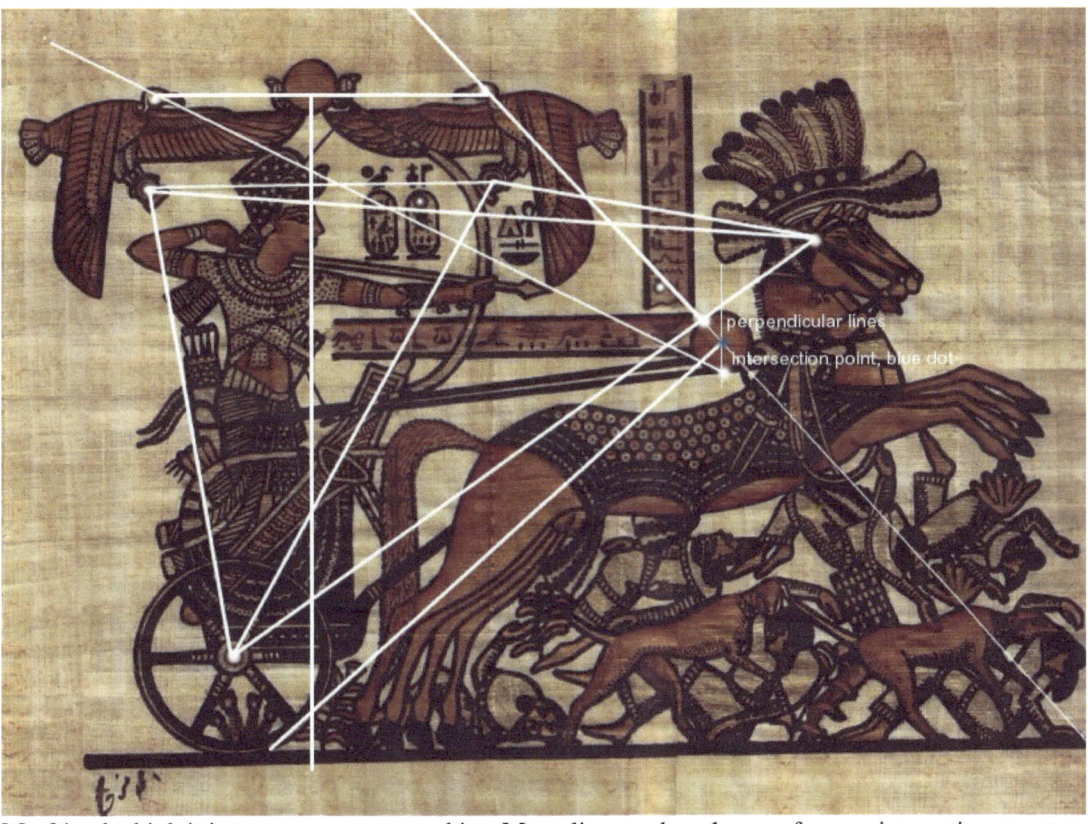

My friends think it is too many space cookies. Many lines and angles can form as interesting structure, often meaningful as RV leads past norms. Possibly descriptive of breakthroughs, and Elsewhere/when relevance. Note the perpendicular from the bottom right end running backwards, also forming a neat triangle using the point where motion would begin at the bottom of the wheel at the bottom left of the View.

Full Perpendicular; 4D perimeter in 2D overlap 3D sided figure. Central point of large Orb (at right), has multi-planar perpendicular/tangent intersection points. Described by extending the view lines outward according to the central positions of the two top left birds eyes, and the lower central perpendicular/tangent of the large Orb (at right). As well as the level Perpendicular, that ends with the tip of the lowermost corner. The very very end point, as it were. The balanced or Omega point to go with the other arrangement of the same large Perpendicular, the line that ends at the beginning, the Alpha point, of motion of the underneath of the wheel. Incredibly arranged and yet precision designed. It appears complicated but comes out merely complex. They are like Story Math.

   A page from the original work. Sometimes it was quite the chore to separate out the info later. Hopefully a visual describing teleports in the future? Always hopeful…it includes, oddly enough, the two ancient Egyptian elements from the word Range. The two matching semi-circles. Along with a pair of legs to indicate motion.

I used to make these things called rainbow makers out of the clear glass using a tiffany copper foil method. There is one slant, that in particular, will create a surface of tension on the surface of the water, such that even turned upside down, the open hole at the top, of some size, will not release. The water does not drip out. It only works with the precise angles and shit. It has to be just right. I make lots of them, and only ok, maybe twice, did it get it. It is of course a normal although unusual state, with a physical explanation. But it is a wonderful example of how the seemingly abnormal or paranormal is just a precision alignment of conditions, an Illusion, not ghosts or mysterious forces. Just, *dynamics*…that allow for the suspension of the regular or norm of the state of matter. Usually, and most often, the water will flow out of the hole. As a drip or a full run, it doesn't just sit in air. But, yes, it can. That would be an example of physical matter behaving in a *magical* or seemingly inexplicable or irregular state. Illusion, based on Reality. And no, it is not just like that for a moment like the airs above the ground, in this case it actually holds and the water stays.
Cohesive surface tension; simple, natural applied physics, dependent on the specific dynamics involved.

You can think of this process in much the same manner. It is not always, but only during the times that at the quantum levels, (exhibited by Feynman and others), there is a dynamic cohesive state, enabling for a particular freeze moment to link to, to include in the View Theme, as a pattern or emote. The rare but entirely possible, that allows for us to get a grid map of precision points, or dots of the 5th, present in the now. Present and within our own understanding, as to regular timelines. The new info is not glowing or anything unusual. It is merely here now, as a wave packet of info, (however expressed or revealed) not just occurring by linear timeline as else-when.

Hence, precog. The decoding of these into usable info is not a match of one to one but like an overall outline, composed of details. An artistic discipline in itself, just to perceive the value in the View Theme. Sorting out from all the unessential clutter and static. Tuning in, and strengthening already forming as certain, the future lines thus perceived ahead. It is only the Probable and Certain not the almost or could have been. This is the Real Future, that is brought forward, there is only speculation in regards to our understanding and interpretation not the actual freeze moment or wave packet's info itself. That is certainty exemplified here, since a wave packet of given's make up a View Theme. Otherwise it would be chaos and random impulses and a decidedly nonsensical Universe.

The glass studio I used to work for in the East, made Rainbow Makers, a many sided glass and tiffany foiled and soldered object that once filled with water, the sun would shine through to create colourful light spectrum prisms. Apparently cohesive forces on a liquid surface act at the tangent to the edge or outer limit defining the surface. On an even surface the forces are balanced at all points equally. If the angle between the material and the tangent to the liquid surface, or angle of contact is greater than ninety degrees, adhesive forcers overrule cohesive, and water will rise up to *wet* the glass. It seems this glass and water article has the surface tension conditions necessary for acting like a wedge or block, tight at its outer rim or edges, not allowing for any give or motion at all of the water, hence no drip, as per these photos.

In effect, defying gravity. Causing a condition of suspension with the heavier substance remaining over the lighter substance with nothing but tension setting the limit. Now, how this is involved otherwise, I am sure it is beyond me. Something tells me if someone had more understanding of the physics, this particular tale or story line in the View Theme would be revealing a lot more. With my limited learning, I am doing good to pick up on the end of the thread, the start of the trail. Is this then a hint or glimpse of a message that requires further study to get an anti-gravity force or quantum dynamic ability set in motion for star travel?

Rainbow Maker, Stained Glass Tiffany method, water filled clear glass; open top, drip-less when inverted; all entirely within our normal physical dimension's constraints.

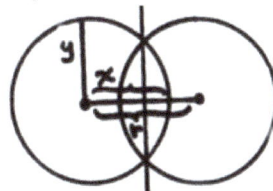 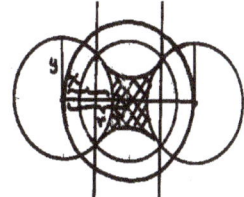

       Diagram 1   Diagram 2

diagram 2 is just diagram 1 mirrored again to the right.

Within these 4D collapsed down to 2 D renderings, this is a standard technique, of perspective, nothing magical nor startling involved, this defined area of workable mechanics involving light speed and its perceivable and measurable effects.

Lorentz equation adjustments are needed near light speed, but Minkowski diagrams allow for reflecting spacetime equations, with adequate considerations for describing realtime effects. With some slick manipulations you can come up with the above (my pigeon set), form of the equation, other variations on the theme are popular. online, that then needs to be set to zero for the freeze frame moment. Bringing the 5th-D info into the visually descriptive (diagram capable) familiar 4th D.

The movie 'Thin Red Line' has a couple of View match links showing between the fighters and the Japanese landscape. Also, there was a battle scene where a few explosions occurred near and at the top of a ridge, that are described visually in the Chariot View. Now, the area immediately behind it, has the wavy thick ridgework, that I had set, also, (multiple links and superimposed details are also working in a View), as the mammoths from 10,000. B.C. Now, in the movie, when the explosions were occurring, the surrounding area had sloping hill ground work ridges that were a visual match, to the 'mammoths' wavy lines. To the right of this area, outlined by white dots, is another area I have enlarged, and found within the empty space, the outline of an urn, or vessel of sorts, is the descriptive tale of the 20 fragments of comet Shoemaker-Levy 9, hitting Jupiter successively, in July 1994. The row of dots showing here, gets progressively smaller, describing a journey, and to their right is the curved eye or Giant Red Spot swirling continuously on this huge planet. Described as a large dot, seen clearly although partially, below.

    Also shows as a string of sharp objects orbiting a large object in the center, the darkened side of the beard, being now limited to being seen as only the outer, and on, in terms of absolute space, this line being a radius (diagram 3.)The lower right bottom has an arc form, like the bow with one arrow, dividing it, and above this is a triangular shape, maybe a ship heading into the dot, er, shape for planet, Jupiter or otherwise. The bow and arrow form is in purple dots, and the possible ship is outlined in blue dots. The large black dot, (like the Shoemaker-Levy 9 comet strike visual) being again representative of a planet. Refer to the photos of August, 2008 when Jupiter was being hit by Shoemaker-Levy 9, July 1994. Matches the row of progressively larger dots here forming the band of dots around the man's head (sideways).

    (5) The method and aim being the bow, and the dot combined with the darker radius line extending outwards from it, within the circular section of the orbit, described here too, the hieroglyphic letter for T. the dot and the line, forming the part of the letter found in the Rongo Rongo script that matches to the Egyptian letter that I pulled out, as distinctly linked. A match. Only, here the shape is reversed and done as a negative image, it is black inside the dot, not open like in the Rongo Rongo form. Same shape, same letter, though. For visual view matching. The white dots are outlining the shape of the letter for T.

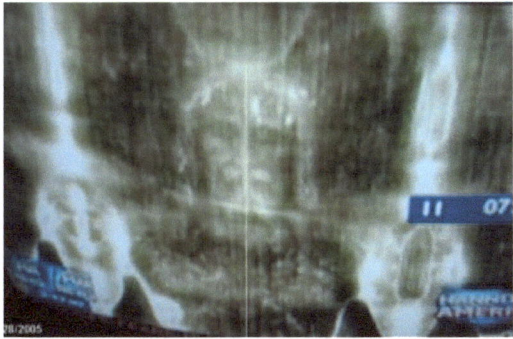  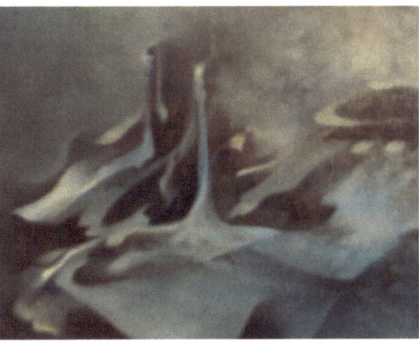

Turin Shroud; timelight 5th D lines; Remote View painting 2005

  1.  2.  3.   4.

1. Jupiter hit by comet fragments Shoemaker-Levy 9. 2. Idealized crystal/magnetic pattern.
3. Cross/Flag 4. View of arrow head (also match to shape under cross) and real arrow head.

Remote Viewing , the 5th and Quantum Chromo Dynamics -
(28 Feb. 2007) Excerpt up at CERN on the web:
Controlled Quantum State Transfer in a Spin Chain
By Jiangbin Gong (1) and Paul Brumer (2), (1) Department of Physics and Center for Computational Science and Engineering, National University of Singapore
(2) Chemical Physics Theory Group and Center for Quantum Information and Quantum Control, University of Toronto, Toronto, Ontario, Canada. Dated -Oct. 25, 2006
-…in this paper we first show that by optimizing a particular transport property using quantum superposition states comprising only a few spins (e.g., four or five), wavepacket pairs with some highly desired features emerge automatically from the ensuing dynamics. We then demonstrate that by applying a sequence of pulsed parabolic magnetic fields one can manipulate these wavepackets, stopping them and later relaunching the travelling wavepackets without individually addressing the spins. As shown below, the stopping, followed by relaunching, can in principle perfectly preserve the quantum information being transferred. This is made possible by taking advantage of powerful relationships between controlling spin dynamics and controlling quantum diffusion dynamics in a paradigm of quantum chaos. -After some detail, it states- …proves that at the end of the stopping time all properties characteristic of an *unknown* quantum wave packet can be exactly restored. This exact re-phasing indicates

that the dynamical evolution associated with the ….in addition to offering a dynamical barrier to stop the quantum transport, precisely reverses the evolution associated with the. As such, the stopping is entirely *non-destructive*, as long as the system is not subject to noise effects during the stopping process. Evidently then, wavepacket assisted information transfer can be perfectly relaunched as the kicking field is turned off.

(They have pulses worked out and other fine details only they are up on, I assure you. I just go for the gist of the thing, more than anything else. Try to see if it fits with my perceptions from actual experience.)

And, from the conclusion:

'…can be applied to the control of spin wave packet propagation and hence the control of propagating quantum information encoded in wave packets. Specifically, we have proposed a simple approach to wave packet creation in a Heisenberg spin chain and demonstrated the possibility of stopping and relaunching information transfer without individually addressing spins or turning off spin-spin interactions….'

What I was calling Quanta, they are calling Wavepackets I think. And they seem to be able to manage control that is precision oriented, and stoppable and re-startable with no perceivable *changes*. I imagine this is quite the feat in Quantum Land. It might explain why I was so easily able to do a Jump to a particular spot and then repeat it precisely so many years later. Never mind the distance involved. Remarkable feats of precision space/time linking seem to be naturally a part of Remote Viewing. Achievable entirely by virtue of the regular processes involved in Quantum's dynamics. This ability to start and stop while preserving entirely, information wavepackets, perhaps is associated with what is glimpsed in part by the above work.

And since the spins that ordinarily matter, are apparently not involved. It would seem that might have some bearing on the effect we see in the Views. I wonder if it is what has come to be called the *Compass Rose*. The Multi-directional facet to a View. Where up becomes down and mirror effects hold true more often than not. Repeat without change. A -stop- considered to be similar to the time duration between my Jump one to the Endurance Crater rock on Mars, and the Jump two about seven years later, to the same rock.

In my View paint of Mars. The direction of the View, looking towards the face, was the same both times. Indicating that this View was precision controllable in terms of direction (spin). Maybe painting or writing a View could be described as -the manipulation of material, to reflect the sensations/waves picked up on, or tuned into, of the information contained within a quantum wavepacket.

As evidenced by the ease of the ability of a Viewer to return and perform a linked View to the same spot that many years apart.

Or, as shown by the completeness of the storyline that often appears to be built-in to the manipulated material (such as paint) used to capture or describe such a mini-theme. A View Theme is really just a composition of many smaller packages of stories or mini-themes merging to form an overall message. Messages received by deciphering the signals attuned to by empathic ability.

   Not to underestimate the direct and essential nature of the sense of tuning into the waves in their packets. A View requiring Empathy to resolve adequately for recording and translating. It is one thing to see something, or hear something. It is something else again, to be able to accurately understand what sensations we are experiencing. Especially with all our own baggage each of us bring to these mere representations of reality. Painting a View Theme is one thing. Reading it is quite another thing, as is un-Veiling, as it reveals.

   The means to selectively bond and realize the spirit and tone accompanying a theme or message, inherent with each unfolding View. We develop our understanding by Reading a sorted out version of meaning from these info-packed wavepackets. Using of course, intuitive-logic, psi and skill to follow the trail of messages involved in forming a comprehensive View Theme.   I believe teleports are a next best leap, given the state of quantum and Views. Probably done, and just fussing over their color. Could you ever see the makings of the fine beginnings of Teleports there, though eh? Unchanged info wave packets, pretty much what you want to achieve to move your molecules around.

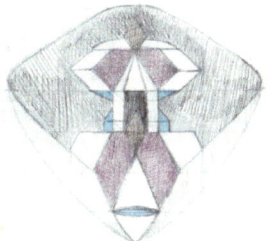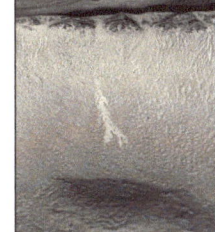

Possible Hieroglyph for Teleport; RV graphic time linked to Mars surface photo of water trail ; flags pre War Games, another necessary component of exploration, the honourable Knights. paint View of a Stealth aircraft but in typical RV descriptive fashion it didn't register the Stealth it just recorded the lines on the runway; View lines; Nuclear terrorism, linked to 'thunder dome' image

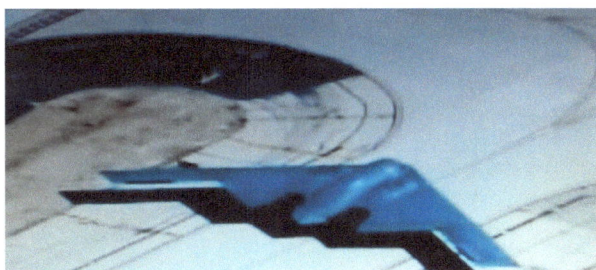

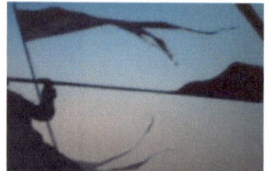 

'Kingdom of Heaven' movie, Crusader flags; match to rear, Chariot RV

RV arrows/flag shape attached; View 2006, Apache Attack helicopter; enlarged snip (lower left, between dots), reversed and together, forming a rib structure

unaltered! They make it sound easy. Might be. I don't have any trouble and I View millions of light years away. In the past and in the future. Remarkably precise Jumps. So, it is not likely t=c, but it is t inseparable from light, like space is inseparable from time. Time is linked to space and light. Even in between light sources in the darkest regions of space, there are waves traveling in some form or fashion or other. It isn't just 'void' since it registers as something, that's why they call it dark matter. Unseen.

They seem to be doing physics here. Theoretical physicists would get way more out of this than me. I can just make out enough to know it was not unsophisticated.

Divine booth or Teleport? The flag marks it as divine. The Claim of Mars, using two Leaps to the same place, with View paintings as claim Flags, portrays the essence of teleportation. Basic Leap as *a from b to c. the same leap point regardless of time=when of leap.* A condition of 'no change' or 'same position/state' is basic when involving quantum.

In regards to how to interpret or decode the RV in order to understand a reading, you would have to look at the entirety. Like the contents in a time capsule. The full page, for a reading. Not an isolated sentence or opinion or prediction or impression. It is not a single card in a Tarot deck kind, although they can be, that, too. Like other oracles, and future telling methods. But, usually, it is the overall and how it links together with the circumstances surrounding the time of its relevance. There is a cohesive element to a View like there is to Holograms. Same as a view piece. That's why I call them View Themes. They are complex, within a simple and defining limit. They are structured Views. I think that is the meaning of the single darkened line under the Chariot View. They tell a tale, and show sights, about the future and the past and 'at times'. they do not just smudge it all together. Although, when you're looking for a specific piece of 'tales about a trip' or other, it sure can seem like it. Just jumbled chaos, random snippets, captured out of a flowing media. Like when I take a snapshot of the individual stills, by pausing a television screen pvr recording and taking a photo. There is no damage to the television, or the show's pattern, it doesn't disrupt anything. But, it does manage to pluck a nice single still frame, or freeze motion frame, of the show that was streaming by. However, when you are attempting to understand a Reading, or View as described by a Remote Viewer, you can not just go in and select one thought or one word to present a match. Things do link and they do match, there can be and is a one to one correspondence at times, but it is not exclusive.

That same point may be and usually is, also completely in synch, by the Czech Doll Boxes and pattern recognition links, thus being shared with other relevant points. Identical and/or descriptive. The View paintings are not full of points that read one way, and that way only. Although, at times, given the also available precision links, they do show a characteristic of oneness or complete individuality by virtue of the sense of cohesiveness to a subject or object. They can be seen one way, as a match, without ruling out other matches, other links, other valid meanings coming into play. Not one and only one, but a one as one, that allows for others. A more holistic nature to any part of a View. Likely a result of the multi dimensional aspect. We have to compress it down to see it. The 5th is retrieved by a sense, but shared by a reduced version. The selection of painting as a method, is very much enabling a view of 3D using an essentially 2D means, and limited as such. It doesn't require special handling other than me to keep from smudging it. It doesn't make great light shows or glow. Although in all fairness, paint can do some great little effects. But they are limited to the constraints of their medium, the material they are made of. There is no active Magical component. They are as dead as any other canvas with paint on it. This is a fact. If you find regular reality boring, don't quit your day job for this. Or, let me say, you have to provide your own special effects. Minkowski's time/space diagrams also take 4D, that is just the regular 3 with time as inseparable, and requiring treatment in their equations. So, you take 4D and then collapse it down visually into 2D, or a diagram of such, on a page, in order to have a workable sheet to discuss mathematical constructions, with. Useful as a mapping guide system in order to explore the 5th and play around in SpaceTimeLight glimpsing ahead while still accurately reflecting reality.

Given the advanced RV of ancient Egypt, and the prolific amount of reference to prophecy in the Christian Bible, as well as the visuals of the early scripts and the reference in the early scriptures, it is possible there is an inseparable link between these facilities of ancient prophecy and the modern Remote Viewing 5th D. Views present themselves as cohesive units of time, thought and language interwoven with spirit and heart. Time as an ocean, not a string, not a ruler; psi can sail time as smoothly as it transverses 5th D with its SpaceTimeLight Quantum Leaps.

Ancient Links & Future Trails — First Viewer 5th D

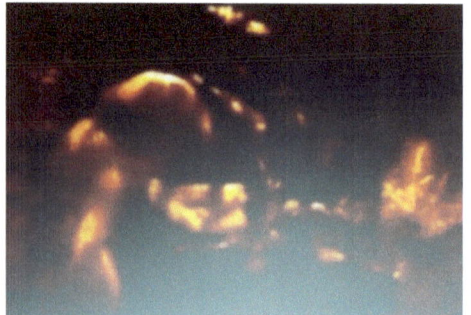

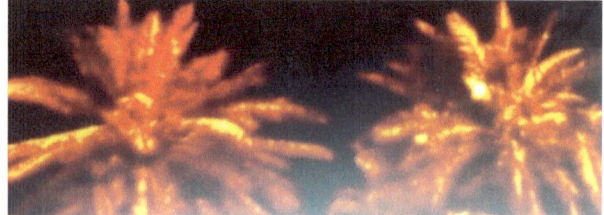

Photo of modern warrior Iraq '06; match enlarged from RV painting; emote for 'WIN

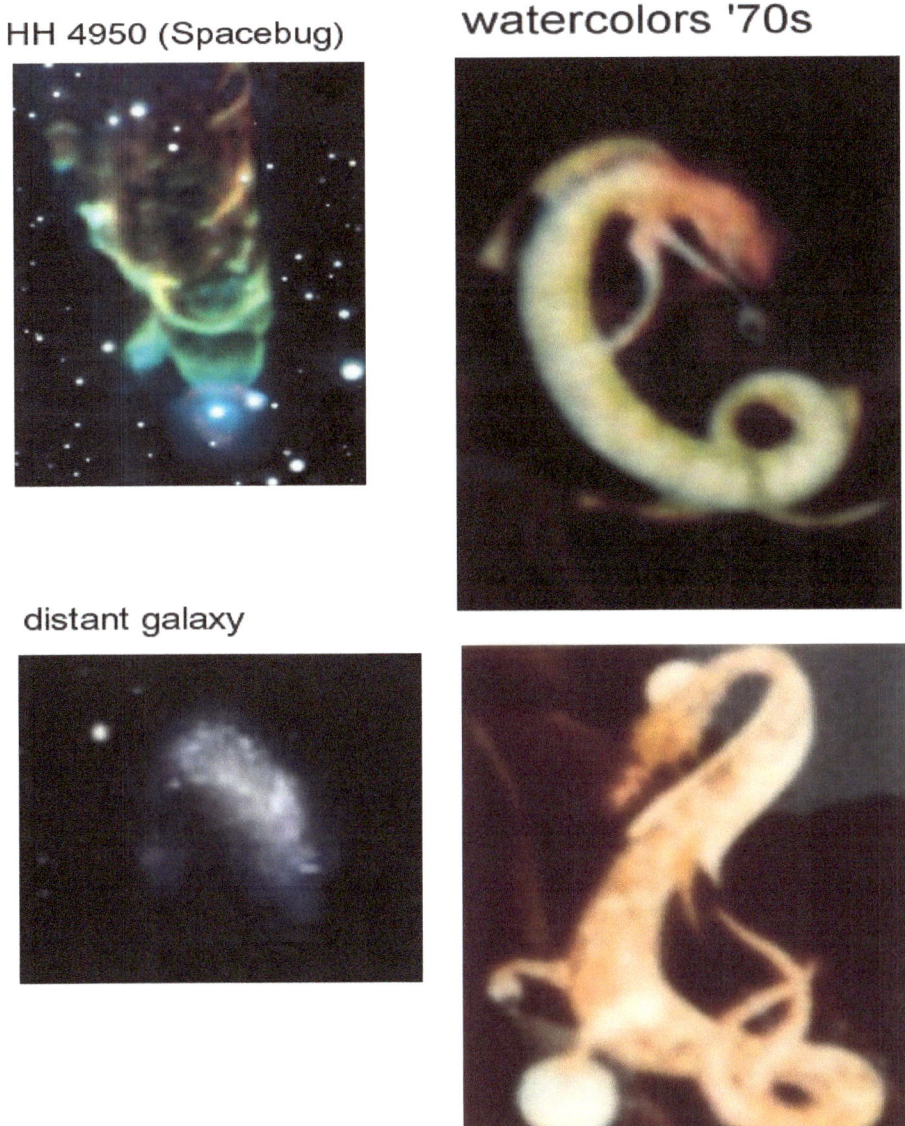

Deepside Q5 Leap Remote Views

www.nuts4mars.com

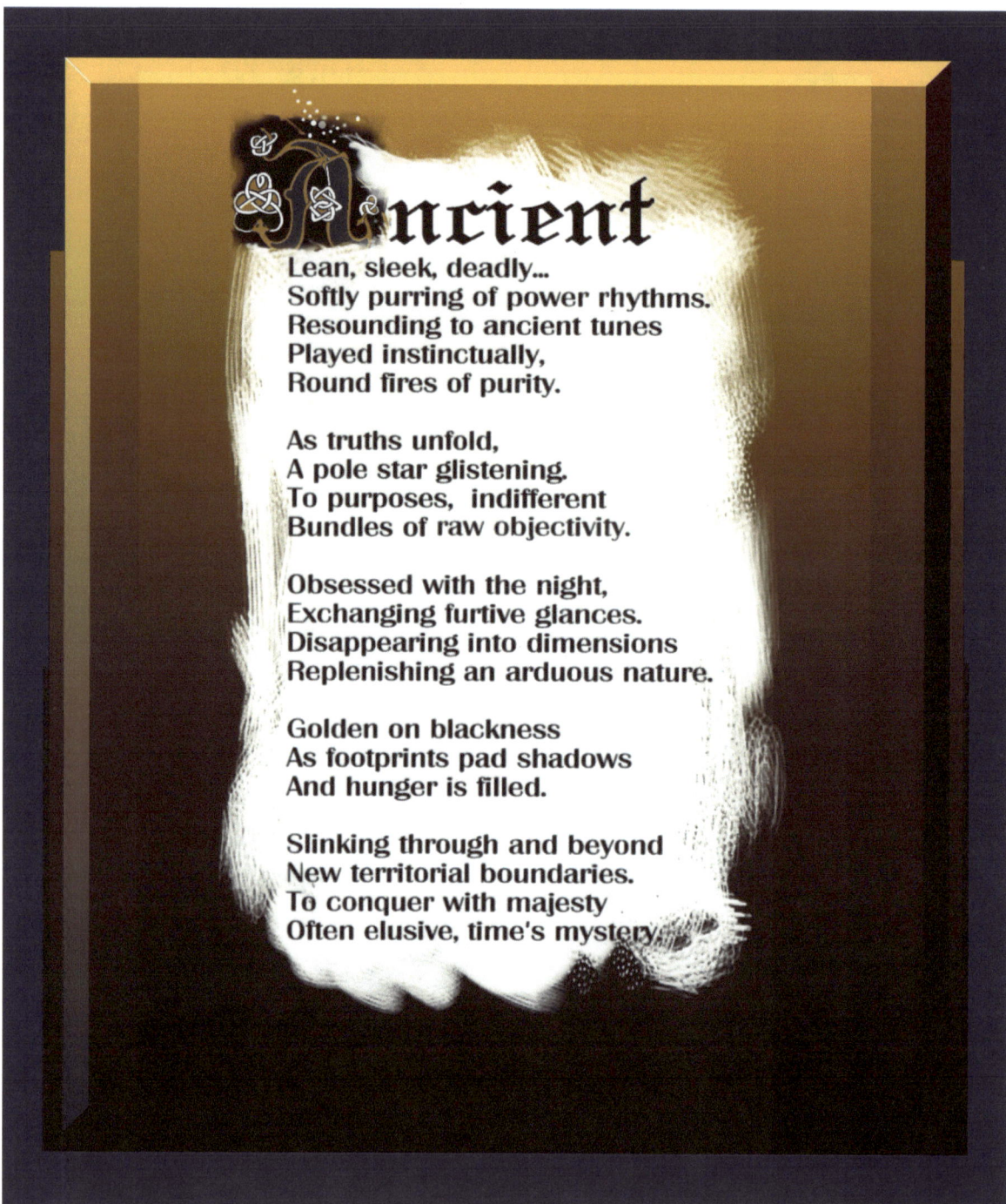

Ancient

Lean, sleek, deadly...
Softly purring of power rhythms.
Resounding to ancient tunes
Played instinctually,
Round fires of purity.

As truths unfold,
A pole star glistening.
To purposes, indifferent
Bundles of raw objectivity.

Obsessed with the night,
Exchanging furtive glances.
Disappearing into dimensions
Replenishing an arduous nature.

Golden on blackness
As footprints pad shadows
And hunger is filled.

Slinking through and beyond
New territorial boundaries.
To conquer with majesty
Often elusive, time's mystery.

www.ingramcontent.com/pod-product-compliance
Lightning Source LLC
Chambersburg PA
CBHW041551220426
43666CB00002B/34